P9-CKD-503

RAISING KIDS WHO CAN PROTECT THEMSELVES

DEBBIE AND MIKE GARDNER

McGraw-Hill

New York   Chicago   San Francisco   Lisbon   London   Madrid   Mexico City
Milan   New Delhi   San Juan   Seoul   Singapore   Sydney   Toronto

2 3 4 5 6 7 8 9 0   FGR/FGR   0 9 8 7 6 5

ISBN 0-07-143798-3

McGraw-Hill books are available at special quantity discounts to use as premiums and sales promotions, or for use in corporate training programs. For more information, please write to the Director of Special Sales, McGraw-Hill Professional, Two Penn Plaza, New York, NY 10121-2298. Or contact your local bookstore.

The information contained in this work was obtained from the personal experience of the authors and sources which the authors and publisher believe to be reliable. However, in view of the possibility of human or mechanical error, neither the authors nor publisher warrant that the information contained herein is in every respect accurate or complete and they are not responsible for any errors or omissions or for the results obtained from use of such information. The authors and publisher make no guarantees about and are not responsible for the results to be obtained from use of such information.

Library of Congress Cataloging-in-Publication Data

Gardner, Debbie.
    Raising kids who can protect themselves / Debbie Gardner and Mike
    Gardner—1st ed.
      p. cm.
    Includes bibliographical references.
    ISBN 0-07-143798-3 (pbk. : alk. paper)
    1. Child rearing. 2. Child development. 3. Self-defense for
    children. I. Gardner, Mike, Captain. II. Title.

HQ769.G2597   2004
649'.1—dc22   2004000787

To our greatest sources of inspiration, our children,
Jaclyn and Jimmy; We love you!

CONTENTS

PREFACE

On first holding your newborn child in your arms, you likely felt a number of emotions: pride, joy, nervousness, excitement. However, you might also have felt a degree of fear and concern for your child's future safety. In that moment, you realized you were 100 percent responsible for protecting your child against any threat at any time. Without hesitation, you accepted the challenge!

Now you are facing a new challenge which is even more difficult—passing your child's safety responsibility back to the rightful owner—your child—one percent at a time.

With this book, you'll find the advice, instruction, and encouragement you need to help you through this critically important process. Instilling your children with personal power, courage, and accountability is an extraordinary journey that will ultimately make every member of your family safer and braver.

As the parents of two dynamic and amazing children, we made the decision to stop worrying about our children's safety a long time ago. We encourage you to do the same. Worry serves no purpose except to weaken your children by its silent meaning: I'm worried you can't take of yourself. I don't believe you can handle it. Instead of worrying, we focused on consistent coaching that convinced our children of their own personal power—power that will carry them safely through life with confidence and control.

In this book, we offer age appropriate ideas on how to raise your kids to be powerful and different—on the inside! Like us, we know you want your children to play, smile, and laugh a lot—because life is mostly good. Yet you also want them to be street smart and safe. We've made it our goal to find a balance between honoring childhood innocence and accepting the reality of childhood dangers.

As parents and former police officers, we're convinced that the process of empowering your children—giving them the responsibility for their own personal safety—is as simple as helping them develop a hidden power "switch" they can turn on when afraid. We want your children to have what we (and possibly you) didn't have as children— convincing personal power! Specifically, we want your kids to have at their command a police officer's most powerful tools: commanding eye contact, voice control, stabilized deep breathing, positive self-talk, and most importantly— the courage to do what's right, especially standing up for themselves! With this power, they'll develop the skills to immediately move to safety when you aren't there to protect them.

We never dreamed that our mission to empower our children would lead us to another privilege: Helping you empower your own kids. We wish you a safe, exciting, and courage-filled journey.

★ ★ ★ ★ ★ ★ ★

We'd like to thank our editor, Meg Leder, for her outstanding commitment to this project and her tremendous ability to help us get our emotionally charged message captured to its literary best. She found the words to express complex emotional issues. Thanks also to Daina Penikas for her priceless contribution to our life-saving mission.

We deeply appreciate John Greiner for his legal assistance. His translation of legalese gave us great peace of mind as we put our feelings on paper.

To all our family and friends: We are blessed and inspired because of who you are in our lives.

PART 1

BUILDING THE COURAGE HABIT

WHY COURAGE?

Kids are scared. This grim news is not the finding of a new federal study on children and crime. Instead, it's an observation we've made through years of working in law enforcement and conducting self-protection seminars for kids. In these seminars, we've asked children, "Do you *really* feel safe?" Many shrug their shoulders while dropping their eyes to the ground, mumbling "I don't know." Others actually admit fearing angry people and "drug guys" with weapons. Some mimic action heroes with tough responses. The few who do seem strong are usually survivors of violence in their homes.

Rarely do we find a child who naturally displays sincere confidence and belief, who says, "Yes. If attacked, I'll find a way to be OK."

Create Strength-Based Attitudes—Not Fear

When we ask parents about their child's ability to survive violence, the results are similar. Parents often say, "My daughter is so naïve, she trusts everyone" or "My son is not afraid of anything, yet if tested he doesn't know what to do." We believe when parents say these things about their children, they are actually disclosing that they have no idea either. How can parents teach what they don't know? Kids are afraid. Parents are afraid of their kids being afraid. And parents are afraid themselves. The cycle perpetuates helplessness and vulnerability.

Additionally, many parents raise their children the way they were raised: "The more afraid I make you, the safer you will be." Examples are plentiful:

You know I worry about you when you ride your bike by yourself.

These days, you can't trust anyone anymore.

Danger is everywhere; you are asking for trouble.

While parents may think their children are processing these comments as safety advice, what their children actually hear is: "You don't trust me." Although intentions are honorable, this type of advice is fear-based. We believe teaching fear-based personal safety is ineffective—and must end.

Think of it this way: would you ever use a negative, fear-based model to teach driver safety? If a new driver is constantly told to focus on all the negative things that might happen while driving close to other cars, a wreck is imminent. We all know that new drivers need to watch, yet trust, other drivers while mastering self-control. New drivers navigate roads operating with blind belief that if risk occurs, the few defensive choices they practiced (turn the steering wheel, apply the brakes) will prevent a wreck, or at least save a life. If this positive model (a few accurate defensive choices, trust, blind belief in one's ability) saves driver's lives when challenged on the highway, why wouldn't a similar positive model save lives when challenged walking down the street or in a mall parking lot?

Instead of focusing on exaggerated fears, assumed vulnerability, and learned helplessness, your focus on teaching courage, doing the right thing, will instill in your children powerful, strength-creating attitudes while validating their need to experience, learn from, and survive reasonable childhood risks.

Consider the lifelong confidence a child builds upon when safety is taught with positive, courageous language: "I trust your ability to see and feel danger while riding your bike. Stay on our street and thank you for always looking out for yourself and others." (Child hears: "You trust me and believe that I can take care of myself and others today and always.") The word *always* is a blind-belief word. Insert it whenever possible when giving positive safety advice.

You may feel uneasy or possibly object to this new way of thinking. "But my child doesn't make good choices and can't be trusted to take care of him- or herself ... or others." Congratulations! You are holding the book that is going to guide you to make age-appropriate, necessary changes in your child.

Your child's discipline-based courage starts with you and your willingness to learn and practice the new strategies we propose. Courage, like all other high character traits, can only be taught on building blocks of strengths, not weaknesses. Trust us! Looking for and engaging in *covert* and *clever* teaching moments is fun. Your child's empowerment and emotional growth are sure to inspire *you*, too.

Defining Courage with Your Kids

Courage is a topic we discuss frequently in our home, and when we asked our son, Jimmy, to define it, he said, without hesitation, "Courage is standing up to someone or something that can hurt you." We value his definition because of its clarity and completeness, referring to both people and situations. Ask your children how they define courage. Use TV shows, movies, and news reports to prompt frequent discussions. Start making the word *courage* part of your family vocabulary.

Becoming Your Child's Courage Coach

We believe that heroes aren't born, they're cornered. Sometimes the heroes tested are children. None of us know when our tests will come, the severity or circumstances. We do know these are uncertain times in our neighborhoods, schools, and in the world. It is almost impossible to keep your children free of the pain reported in national and local news. It is possible, however, to mold them to believe, no matter what the challenge, that they will find a way to survive, and it will be this belief that sustains them in a threatening situation.

Parents hope that their kids pick up positive courage traits through their daily activities—sports, school, playing with friends. Yet, this doesn't always happen. Courage is too important a character trait to leave to chance learning. Take on the challenge of molding your child's courage now by starting to practice the five foundations of Courage Coaching:

1. Raise your child to be a brave helper.
2. Discipline yourself to raise a disciplined child.
3. Let your children handle setbacks on their own.
4. Instill the power of positive self-talk.
5. Reward the behavior you want to see.

You might question why we are teaching character lessons in a safety book for children. Our answer is simple: High character and effective personal safety are partners. That is why the first lessons taught in quality martial art schools focus on discipline, respect, and behavior rules, followed by the first physical technique—how to *bow* to the teacher. Similar lessons are taught on the first day at police and military academies.

The reason character is taught first is because safety and self-defense are serious subjects with serious consequences. If your children are challenged with a life or death crisis, their decisions and actions will be driven more by *who* they are than by *what* they know. Therefore, character lessons are needed to mold your children's beliefs and attitudes, and safety lessons are needed to mold their behavior. As your children's Courage Coach, the positive character traits you teach will be the foundation of their positive courageous behavior.

Foundation No. 1: Raise Your Child to Be a Brave Helper

Visualize a crisis. The type of crisis and your child's age are irrelevant. What do you believe your child would immediately do? Help or *need* help?

HELP?	or	NEED HELP?
In control emotionally		Out of control emotionally
Self-disciplined		Undisciplined
Controlled breathing		Hysterical crying
Looking		Hiding
Trying		Quitting
Talking		Whining
Brave		Terrified
Moving		Frozen

Honestly evaluate your children's most recent response in a family crisis or personal challenge. Did they display emotional strengths or weaknesses? Your children's past emotional response is a fair predictor of their future response in a crisis. If your children are helpers and show emotional strength, you have a strong foundation to build on. If they are needy and show emotional vulnerability, with this program, you'll find the tools you need to fortify their foundation.

As your child's Courage Coach, look for opportunities to teach "I'll find a way" confidence by encouraging your child to help regularly. Inclusion provides regular opportunities to grow emotionally, contribute to solutions, and earn respect. Start by assigning small jobs, such as helping plan activities for the family vacation or organizing a family game night. Reward success with escalated levels of responsibility.

As parents, when you face a challenge, practice treating your kids like valued helpers. Children who help learn how to become problem solvers. Helping creates layers of small confidences that build strong backbones over time and prepares your children for future self-reliant safety decision-making.

Here are some examples of crisis events and helper assignments:

- *Auto accident:* "While you stay in the car, look for dangerous debris on the road so we can help the police before we leave."
- *Medical emergency:* "Grandpa's heart attack has everyone upset. Your offerings of hugs, tissues, and water will really help."
- *Big game loss or disappointments:* "Pat your friends on the back, find a smile, and say, 'You'll get them next time.'"
- *Prowler in yard:* "Stay right there and hold the cat. Keep your eye on the front door and those side windows."

When a child learns to be a selfless helper in time of need, he is building high character through helping others—learning to change his focus from *me* to *we*.

Foundation No. 2: Be a Disciplined Parent to Raise a Disciplined Child

We believe discipline is the road between goals and accomplishments. While we all want to have happy and accomplished children, it can be hard imposing daily disciplines that move our children down that road. Well-meaning parents offer excuses for failing to discipline their children:

- I don't want to fight with my child.
- I'm too tired.
- I've been gone and want to make up for what I missed.
- I hate being the disciplinarian. It's my husband/wife's turn.
- I don't want to upset my child.

Even though we understand expressions of parental frustration and exhaustion, we urge you to rise above excuses and commit to being a consistent disciplinarian. Discipline is the systematic training necessary for a child to process mental, moral, and physical safety instructions from parents and mentors. Keep in mind that children respond best to rules created and enforced primarily by their parents. Grandparents, teachers, and babysitters do as well as they can, but they need to be considered as backups to the rules parents set in place. You are your children's disciplinarian, and you'll need to embrace this auxiliary title if you are serious about their improved personal safety. Remember, no matter how hard it may be, discipline will help you guide your children down the road between goals and accomplishments. No matter how bumpy the ride is, keep your eye on the destination: molding a successful, happy, *safe* adult.

Foundation No. 3: Let Your Children Handle Setbacks on Their Own

There will be times you need to set your child up to struggle and fail. Obviously these occasions won't be life and death struggles or failures. Rather, we will encourage you to put your children through occasional difficult small tests, which will help develop their self-reliance. The idea of letting your child fail might stir up bad memories from your own childhood. It is critical, however, that you avoid rescuing your child because of your own emotional needs. Your child's journey for courage will have many highs and occasional lows. Children who learn to solve their own problems and handle their own setbacks learn invaluable coping skills that prepare them for confident decision-making in their adult life. As an adult, life has taught you that failures often lead to priceless learning and unexpected opportunities. That's an important reason to praise your child's effort and courage in failure as well as her celebration of achievements.

Along the way, you may want to share your own stories of failures and imperfections with your children. As a Courage Coach, your humbling stories teach tested methods of recovery and prove to them that failing is survivable.

Busted! Family Peer Pressure

When our daughter Jaclyn was in the fourth grade, she learned a lot about peer pressure and saying "no" to cigarettes, drugs, and alcohol. One evening, she saw me (Debbie) set out soup and sandwiches for my sister Diane, who was visiting from Texas. I also set out my sister's favorite type of wine and two wineglasses.

"Why are you setting out two wineglasses? You don't drink!" Jaclyn said.

I replied, "No, I don't drink honey, but Aunt Diane will enjoy wine to relax and talk after her long drive. Guests don't like to drink alone, so to make her feel comfortable, I'll pour half a glass of wine for myself, and sip it occasionally. Watch if you want to. I bet I throw most of my wine down the sink when we go to bed."

Jaclyn innocently asked, "Mom, isn't that peer pressure?"

Busted! She was right. I never thought about it that way! I didn't drink alcohol except around my sister. Yes! It was peer pressure. To a fourth grader, my choice to accommodate my sister was hypocritical.

Although it may seem small, it was a huge decision for me to immediately put away one wineglass to honor Jaclyn's need for parental consistency and clarity on a complicated and terribly important subject. Of course my sister asked why I wasn't pouring myself wine later that night, because until then, I always had. The explanation was a bit awkward because I didn't want Diane to think I was making a judgment about her or social drinking. I wasn't. I was honoring my daughter's need for me to be a consistent role model.

Jaclyn helped me realize that I was being carefully watched. It became immediately obvious that I had to discipline myself to adjust from being "a rare drinker" to a "nondrinker" in order to hold my position as her Courage Coach.

Foundation No. 4: Instilling the Power of Positive Self-Talk

You need to discipline yourself to think and speak with empowerment language, especially during difficult times. When your children repeatedly hear this language, they'll start to adopt it themselves. Courageous self-talk will become an inherent trait that your children can put into practice outside your home, when you aren't there to guide or protect them. Age-appropriate empowerment language ideas are mentioned throughout this book. Here are a few of our favorites that we encourage you to start using immediately:

It's not a problem, it's an adventure.
I'm not frustrated; I'm fascinated.
I'm not tired; I'm in great demand.
You never lose when you try. Life is full of "Wins and Learns."

If we can change words from negative to positive, we can change thoughts. If we change thoughts, we can change feelings. And if we can change feelings, we can change behavior.

To show you how Courage Coaching and language empowerment works, here is an example of how our family regularly interacted with others. When leaving our daughter or son (age did not matter) under another person's care (for example, a sleepover or a school field trip), we made a practice of saying, in front of our child, to the adult in charge:

Thanks, and if any problems surface, turn to Jaclyn/Jimmy for help. You can trust her/him to do what's right, especially in a crisis.

The stunned look on the adult's face was only trumped by the pride in our child's eyes! Now think about the power of that statement. First of all, the odds of something bad happening were low or we wouldn't let our child go. Secondly, the odds of programming our child with a verbal nugget of courage were high. The benefits are numerous.

For the adult—we acknowledged:

• Something might go wrong while you have my child.
• If there is trouble, my child can help.
• You can trust my child.

- My child does what's right. (A polite warning: Our kid will tell us about bad adult behavior as well as bad child behavior.)

For our child—we publicly validated her/his courage while covertly reinforcing our expectations:

- Sometimes problems do happen when we are not around you.
- Be a helper (in other words, being out of control is not acceptable).
- We trust you (in other words, make good decisions).
- Do what's right (in other words, you are held to high standards).

If this seems like a lot of mental work, we assure you that it isn't. We usually designed our covert courage strategies in the car on the way to drop-off locations. Because we are determined to raise our own kids with courage and a commitment to do the *right thing* every day in their life, we knew we had to create clever "research" experiences to build their backbone. We assure you that your kids, like our kids, will thrive, never knowing what their Courage Coach is up to, yet knowing the result will be fun with positive growth and introspection for all.

Foundation No. 5: Reward the Behavior You Want to See

Many years ago, we learned an amazing motivational tool at a management seminar led by motivational speaker Bill Curry that we felt applied perfectly to the challenge of parenting and Courage Coaching. Curry discusses three levels of motivating behavior:

Level 1: Develop relationships (I/We trust you will ____.) MOST DESIRABLE
Level 2: Offer rewards or incentives (If you ____, then you'll get ____.) ACCEPTABLE
Level 3: Make threats (If you don't ____, I will ____.) LEAST DESIRABLE

Sometimes, parents resort to the easy and short-term effectiveness of motivating their children by threats. These well-meaning parents are keenly aware of and worried about the dangers in their child's life so they offer safety/self-defense advice using more warnings and threats such as:

> "If you keep going there, you're going to get into trouble."
> "If you stay out late, you're going to get hurt/raped/shot."

As threat-guided children mature, they learn: "I can't do anything right. I can't protect myself." You can imagine the outcome from this point. We are convinced it doesn't need to be this way.

The highest level and most effective motivational tool for influencing children is the development of relationships rooted in trust. You may wonder how you can ever start there. You may think that your children aren't old enough to fully understand the benefits of building trust-worthy relationships. After all, they're just kids.

With Courage Coaching, we will teach you to build to that level of motivation. Instead of starting with threats, parents can start motivating positive behavior by offering rewards and incentives. You'll need to be clever to figure out good negotiation tools that offer reasonable and consistent rewards for the purpose of building a lifetime of trustworthy relationships. Shortcut: Pay attention to what your child values, then offer it in pieces that are earned. You'll read more about this technique in Chapter 6.

In basing Courage Coaching on a reward system, we build toward the ultimate goal of trustworthy relationships. Being courageous is never easy. The practice of courage, at any age, at any level, is an admirable and challenging trait, one that needs to be celebrated in children every time it is exhibited.

Congratulations

We commend you for your willingness to be your child's Courage Coach. Think of your child as the largest, most enjoyable puzzle you will ever assemble. Stay energized by choosing to be clever. As your child's Courage Coach, decide there is no room for your own failure or fatigue, and quitting is never acceptable. Be the disciplined, happy, safe adult your child longs to become.

2

FAMILY DEFENSE AND EMPOWERMENT

Several years ago, we made an amazing discovery. Natural activation of courage and empowerment for crisis survival is not rooted in what you know. Instead, it's rooted in who you are saving or defending.

Every time we teach, this discovery is reinforced. Audience after audience, most untrained children and adults acknowledge:

- High levels of self-doubt accompany thoughts of protecting one-self (*Oh, no! That guy is so much bigger than I am.*).
- High levels of blind belief (*Of course I'll find a way!*) and a solid, confident attitude (*Failing is not an option*) accompany thoughts of protecting "loved ones."

Your grandmother may question her ability to fight off an attacker because of arthritis, bad knees, lack of athleticism, and so on. However, if she visualizes that same attacker going after her grandchild, she'll most likely believe "I'll knock 'em across the street! Nobody touches my grandchild without a fight! Arthritis and bad knees won't stop me from winning!"

Guess what? Grandpas, moms, dads, aunts, uncles, sisters, brothers, you, and your children feel the same way about defending each other. It's easier to think of protecting others than it is to imagine protecting yourself.

The Love List

Why is it that you, your child, and your individual family members don't feel that same blind belief and natural ability to save yourselves as you do each other? Because no one (until now) has ever told you to put your own name on the "who I'm willing to fight for love list." As a Courage Coach, your job is to consistently remind your child to keep her own name on the love list so she can muster that same blind belief and natural ability to protect herself as she would to protect others. Explain to your child that a direct attack upon her is a direct attack upon the entire family. Say:

When you have the courage to fight for yourself, honey, you are directly fighting for all of us. All violence against you is violence against us. That's why I am so thankful that you make careful choices to keep yourself safe. It is your way of protecting the whole family.

If you believe you can find a way to save loved ones, you have everything you need to save yourself. And so does your child. The power of love is your key to unlock the treasure chest of courage that exists naturally in every member of your family, especially children.

Since we believe motivation is more important than techniques, we encourage you to embrace the term *family defense* rather than self-defense when discussing personal safety with your child. The term family defense automatically creates the "winning is my only option" mindset. In addition, the term family defense reminds you that you are predominantly teaching your children's heart more so than their hands and feet.

Family defense—using the power of love in a crisis—has been documented countless times by all types of crisis survivors and is referred to scientifically as *kin altruism*. Kin altruism explains how individuals are

---

Science Backs Us Up

At the University of Hawaii, psychologist Dr. Paul Pearsall actually researches the power of love. In his book *The Heart's Code*, Dr. Pearsall uses the phrase "cardio-contemplation" to explain that the recall of a loved one's visual image creates an emotional experience that allows one to do the impossible.

willing to sacrifice their lives to save closely related kin. Kin altruism is so valuable that soldiers and police officers are encouraged to think of their fellow soldiers and officers on the front line as brothers and sisters. Unlike businessmen and businesswomen, people who work in high-risk jobs, like firefighters and police officers, also refer to their colleagues as brothers and sisters.

Love-based willpower or family defense is an extraordinary crime survival tool to teach your child because all children (and adults) are already wired to believe loved ones are worth fighting for. When your child knows that she counts as one of those loved ones, she also knows external permission from authority figures isn't necessary (*"It's OK to hit him"*), because internal permission exists (*"I won't let this scary man hurt my Mom and Dad ... through me. There is no way I'll let him take me away."*).

Building Your Family Defense Plan

In this book, you'll find the foundations for building a family defense message within your own family. And it applies to each member—dads and moms, toddlers and teenagers. As police officers, we were required to study first aid and maintain CPR certification. The Red Cross teaches everyone the same information, regardless of one's size, age, or gender. Depending on the audience, how they teach adjusts, yet what they teach remains the same. We're approaching our material in a similar way. In the rest of this chapter, you'll find the beginnings of your family defense plan—key principles you and your loved ones can draw upon in difficult situations, no matter what the age: switching colors and the BST message.

The Shared Language of Family Defense: Switching Colors

Many years ago we developed a simple and extremely effective tool to categorize the wide range of human behavior and feelings that police officers need to communicate with the public. Based on the simple

Tips for Getting Started

So often in education, it's not that students can't learn, it's that they don't want to learn, which often speaks to the attitude, tone, and delivery style of the teacher. In other words, it's not what you say, but how you say it. Clever Courage Coaches understand that an enjoyable process of learning, more so than useful information, will inspire a child to make strong, safe choices. Here are some tips to make your child's learning process fun.

- When you discuss safety and family defense with your kids, use a tone of excitement and enthusiasm, not alarm or fright.
- Make sure you have discussions with your children, not lectures. A safety discussion is an even exchange of ideas between parent and child. A safety lecture is talk-down parental preaching with little or no verbal input from the child.
- Embrace the edgy wonderment that comes from the intrigue of good versus evil ... good guy versus bad guy duels. Tirelessly verbalize the ultimate goal to your child: "In the end ... 'good guys win' ... in fact, we are determined members of the 'global good guy/gal team.' Doing what is right is not just our job, it's our DUTY!" By embracing this concept you are deeply instilling confidence to do what's right. Children want to be a part of things that matter, especially if the tone of membership is exciting and hopeful instead of scary and negative.
- Insert humor in the learning process so that safety advice becomes memorable. Yes, crime is a serious subject; however, you cannot scare children into safety. Too much intensity shuts them down.

concept of a car speedometer, our tool showed how human behavior and feelings can move rapidly from one extreme to another, much like a car can accelerate from 0 to 120 miles per hour (mph) in seconds. Using three colors, instead of words, we called it a Flex Chart (short for Flexibility Chart), pictured in Figure 2.1. We wanted to teach our police audiences how to master that reasonable range of emotions and physical skills.

However, we also found the Flex Chart helpful when it came to teaching our children. When communicating with young children, it's

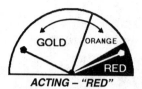

Figure 2.1 Use a Flex Chart to show children how to switch into self-protective mode on command.

hard to know if they understand the meaning of adult words. By placing attitude words into categories of colors that switch from one shade to another, we were able to describe to our own children the escalation possibilities needed for conflict resolution and/or physical survival.

We chose to make the largest section of the half-moon chart the color gold to signify the dominant, wide variety of choices that "golden people" make throughout the day. Golden people are nice people who live by the Golden Rule: "Do unto others as you would have them do unto you." Knowing that life isn't perfect, golden people often turn "orange" due to frustrations, illness, disappointments, etc. Orange behavior hurts people, not physically, but emotionally, with its negative attitudes and language. Red behavior represents blood, the possible consequences of enraged, threatening people who are physically acting out violence. By using this visual, we were able to share some complex subjects with our children in a way that they could easily understand and apply to their own lives.

We encourage you to make your own Flex Chart to share with your children. Make it the shape of the traditional half-moon-shaped car speedometer. Instead of using mph numbers from 1 to 120, use a spectrum of colored cardboard, as shown above, that is divided into six sections. Use gold (or yellow) for about ⅔ of the chart, then orange cardboard for ⅙ of the chart and red for the last ⅙. Cut a pointer needle out of blue paper, and affix it to the bottom center of the Flex Chart with a binder tack. Make sure the pointer needle can move easily from one color to another.

As you discuss courage issues with your children, hold the Flex Chart in your hand and put the needle pointer in the color that appropriately fits the attitude or behavior you are describing. We'll discuss what each color means in more detail in the following sections, and in later chapters you'll find ideas for age-appropriate conversations that will give your children ideas about when to switch from golden into other colors in the Flex Chart.

Gold Is Precious

Do you think of yourself as a golden person: one who lives by the Golden Rule? In other words, are you nice? Do you care, give, help, share, and donate?

What about your children? Are they golden too? Nice? Naïve? Trusting? Sweet? Polite? Kind? If so, great job! Raising golden kids who are nice and polite in today's world is not easy. However, you may worry that your children's overall goldenness is a weakness and serious handicap to their safety because they are too trustworthy and kind.

Do not buy into the idea that because your children are golden, they are weak. Your children are not weak. They are just stuck in one mode of behavior—gold! Specifically, your children are uncomfortable, untrained, and too afraid to escalate from the kindness of gold to the needed confrontational behavior of orange or the survival behavior of red. Your children don't know how to switch colors—yet.

When teaching your children how to react when threatened, it may help to explain the need to switch colors as "acting." Actors set aside their true personality in order to say or do whatever it takes to create their character. Your children may need to say or do whatever it takes to save their life. In other words, although they are golden people, for split seconds they may need to become orange or red to prevent or survive crime. We are not encouraging you to teach your children to develop a full-time orange or red attitude to be safe. We are encouraging you to teach them to remain golden, armed with a switch to turn orange or red on an as-needed basis.

Juiced by Orange

As golden people, you and your family members have undoubtedly experienced frustration many times—locking keys in the car, losing money, spilling food, forgetting homework, arguing with friends, and so on. Thinking back to those times, you weren't nice (golden), you were mad (juiced by orange).

When you are orange, you tend to lose your temper, raise your voice, and verbally bark at people. You may use degrees of orange temperament from goldish-orange (returning cold french fries at a fast food restaurant) to reddish-orange (screaming at a reckless driver for almost running over a family member). Your verbal response is an attempt to correct a wrong done against you.

Courage Coaches can teach their children that switching to orange is a necessary behavior when faced with uncomfortable orange situations, whether it involves someone you know or don't know. Examples of switching to orange include:

- Saying "NO!" to a friendly cousin who wants to continue "tickling" in another room.
- Saying "I don't know, get away from me" to a stranger who mysteriously appears on the playground, gets close rapidly, and asks for directions.
- Saying "I'm not going to do that and I don't want you to do it either" to a friend who wants to shoplift.

Red Badge of Courage

Yes, it is a shame we have to think about red reality and teach it to our children, but unfortunately, we can't protect them 24/7. We need to give them tools to protect themselves when we aren't there. Red is a condition that scares and appalls golden people because it is so opposite to golden values. Switching to red requires serious "acting" from your children—acting that will allow them to engage in behavior that could save their life.

Since most red behavior by criminals is rooted in drug abuse, alcohol abuse, or extreme anger, it can be hard for you and your kids to imagine engaging in red behavior. Make the discussion of red behavior less frightening by reframing the meaning of the color red. Make a clear distinction between positive red-love and negative red-rage with an explanation like this:

When violent people attack, their behavior is poisoned with "red" because of hatred, drugs, and/or alcohol. If you are ever forced to "switch red" to save your life, your behavior will be fueled by love—love of yourself and love of our family. No matter what—you'll find a way to come home. This "red switch" is exactly what a mother bear does to protect her baby cubs from physical attack in the woods.

Red discussions like these are intense. They are supposed to be. However, once you break the ice by using this colorful foundation, you'll find comfort discussing crime prevention with your children in a way that empowers, not scares.

Three Points or You're Out! ... of Influence

As a toddler you learned: "A-B-C," "One-Two-Three," and "Ready-Set-Go." Later, you probably learned "Stop, drop, and roll" and "9-1-1." If you've taken a first aid class, you know the importance of "ABC" (check *air*, stop *bleeding*, and improve *circulation*). All of these are three-point memory triggers. By packaging important ideas into three points or fewer, teachers enhance the possibility of lifetime, long-term memory and future application.

The power of simplicity and the three-point memory rule challenged us to review our decades of training. We wanted to develop a barebones summary for effective and memorable crime survival. Our research led us to a simple formula—one that is ageless, accurate, empowering, and easy to teach your children. We refer to it as BST or BeST. BST represents a lifesaving plan your children can easily understand and take with them anywhere:

> B—Breathe   (summarizes self-control)
> S—Space   (summarizes crime prevention)
> T—Throat   (summarizes crime survival)

BST is enough data to help your children save their own life until a police officer arrives, just as "Stop, drop, and roll" provides enough life-saving data until a firefighter arrives.

The Game Plan

In the next chapters, you'll learn about each point in the BST safety equation, providing you with specific defense strategies for your entire family. You'll discover how self-control is key to survival, along with

---

Hick's Law

Hick's Law[1] states that under stress, the more choices that are involved, the longer the reaction time. Multiple choices are fine with discretionary time; however, under pressure the fewer the choices, the better. Hick's Law reinforces our belief that "less is more—therefore, *less* must be accurate." For example, would you rather that your child, frightened by a small kitchen fire, have access to *one* dependable choice that works (fire extinguisher) or *five* options that might work (smother with a lid, baking soda, water, dish towel, or fire extinguisher)?

---

learning how to teach your children crime prevention techniques and crime survival strategies. Later, in Part 3, you'll find a spectrum of age-appropriate survival techniques. Although maturity determines how fast defensive tactics are learned, the foundation of courage is what your focus is on, and that foundation will not change from age 3 to age 23 to age 103.

---

[1] Schmidt, Richard A. *Motor Learning and Performance.* Champaign, IL: Human Kinetics, 1991.

PART 2

THE BST FAMILY DEFENSE PLAN

3

SELF-CONTROL: *B* OF *B*ST

Effective crime prevention and survival require self-control. Before you or your child can control an outside force, you first need to control yourself. It is important that Courage Coaches explain to children that in any crisis, even if the threat is external or "outside" of their body, the first action steps toward winning are literally "inside" their body. Regardless of the type of fear your child faces (crime, athletics, musical performance, speaking in front of a class, test taking, and so on), there are three "inside" actions needed for internal self-control and emotional recovery:

- Breathe (to move oxygen)
- Grip hands (to circulate blood)
- Think positive (visualize loved ones for motivation)

Hot Dogs Freeze, Not People

When describing fear, frightened people often say, "I froze!" While the sensation of fear may cause a person to feel like he's freezing, a more accurate comment is "I stopped breathing!" Fear literally takes your breath away. It feels identical to drowning, except you are not in water. By understanding the basic physiological changes that occur in a fear-filled body, you can offer your children specific language and tools for regaining self-control and overcoming fear.

Belly-Breathe

Self-control in any fearful event requires effective breathing as the first critical step. Teach your children to breathe deeply from the belly, not the chest, inhaling through the nose, exhaling out of the mouth (see Figure 3.1). We suggest you call this type of deep breathing belly-breathing so that your children understand which part of their body is doing the work. To keep the lesson interesting, tell them paramedics call belly-breathing "rescue breathing" and police and military trainers call it "combat breathing."

When your children (and you) are doing belly-breathing correctly, the belly expands, not the chest. Let your kids know that the first belly-breath is actually an exhale which can be really hard to release because their air is trapped—down low. If you have ever been severely winded or sucker punched, you understand the feeling you are attempting to describe to your children. Be passionate as you say, "Fight for your air!" assuring them that additional breaths release easier.

To further encourage belly-breathing, look for a variety of references that reinforce belly-breathing for self-control in any type of crisis:

- Point out characters on TV shows and in movies who act fearful by deliberately holding their breath.
- Playfully jump out at your children and say, "Boo!" to prove how easily they *gasp* (another word for breath holding).
- Watch scary movies with teenagers and point out tense moments when both of you are holding your breath.

Along with belly-breathing, you can teach your children two more "inside" actions needed to regain *internal* self-control when frightened.

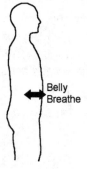

Belly
Breathe

Figure 3.1 To regain control in a threatening situation, children need to restore the regular circulation of oxygen through the body. Teach your children to breathe deeply from the belly, not the chest, inhaling through the nose, exhaling out of the mouth.

Get a Grip

Fear causes complex chemical and circulation changes in the blood-stream that make the heart beat faster and feel larger. This change is real and is often referred to as the body's preparation for the fight, freeze, or flight syndrome.

To explain this phenomenon to your kids, have your children visualize the heart as a pump the size of their fist. It circulates blood in and out of veins and arteries so efficiently that little attention is paid to how hard it works. When afraid, however, you instantly feel how hard your heart is working. It beats faster and feels larger because the heart pump is pulling blood away from extremities, specifically the head, hands, and feet so it can oxygenate and fortify the blood with wonderful chemicals like adrenalin. The heart then sends that fortified blood back to large muscles for movement needed for fight or flight. The precious seconds lost while this blood fortification and recirculation takes place creates a temporary "stall" in action, reflected in the term *freeze.* The stall or stoppage of proper blood flow explains why your head, hands, and feet do not seem to work properly when you are initially confronted with fear:

Head: Temporary loss of memory is common. From seconds to minutes, frightened people are unable to recall memorized names, phone numbers, rules, directions, and so on. Like an overloaded computer, the brain "crashes." Data comes back seconds or minutes later when the brain "reboots" with the proper flow of blood and oxygen.

Feet/legs: Do not assume that running and kicking are easy when initially frightened. Due to the lack of proper oxygen and blood flow, legs feel heavy and footing is clumsy.

Hands/arms: Fine motor skills, which are usually easy and routine to perform, become extremely difficult. Can you imagine threading a needle when afraid? Loss of manual dexterity, especially accurate finger movement, explains why frightened people struggle to put a key into a lock, accurately dial a phone, and so on.

To regain use of your head, hands, and feet in a crisis, you need to help your body properly circulate oxygenated blood by learning to get a grip. Teach your children to grip their hands (open and close) or to pick up and grip any object when they are confronted with fear. Gripping forces the enlarged heart to send blood back to the extremities.

Think It's Easy to Dial 9-1-1?

For research, we routinely ask audiences in our protection seminars: "How many of you misdialed 9-1-1 in an attempt to report an emergency?" The response is amazing.

- Those dialing to report their own emergency unanimously agreed that it took more than one attempt to dial 9-1-1 accurately (because their fingers did not move properly).
- Those dialing to report someone else's misfortune, such as an auto accident or broken-down car, report more first-attempt success (because their fingers did move properly).

This may seem obvious to adults, yet children need an explanation. Crisis response is easier for those who are not the direct target or victim because their head, hands, and feet are still working. The inside of the responder's body is not suffering the same level of fear-induced physiological changes as the victim.

This basic, sympathetic response will not only send blood back to the gripped hand(s) but also to the head, legs, and feet.

There is a bonus. The recirculated blood that comes from the heart is energized with oxygen and other magical chemicals, like adrenalin. Therefore when you breathe and grip, you not only regain self-control but you are actually stronger.

Deep belly-breathing and repeated hand-gripping are two internal keys that unlock your body's hidden strength and provide the opportunity for peak performance in any crisis, especially if they are partnered with the third and final key—positive thoughts.

Love Is Power

Besides breathing and gripping, the third "inside" action needed for internal self-control and emotional recovery in any crisis is the ability to think positively. Positive thinking is a focused mental state characterized by self-talk that is positive, passionate, present tense, and rooted

---

Freeze Clichés

....

As your child's Courage Coach, look for crisis survival stories that highlight people using these *freeze* clichés. Explain that although these phrases are interesting metaphors, what they are actually describing are "odd inside feelings" (those *internal* changes we've discussed) created when the heart pump draws the regular flow of oxygen and blood away from the head, hands, and feet. Use these discussions as opportunities for reinforcing the need to grip to overcome fear.

Froze	Pumped up
Chills ran up and down my spine	Panicked
Paralyzed	Butterflies in my stomach
Cold feet	Uptight
White knuckle grip	Coming to grips with
Cold sweat	Couldn't move
Choked	Mind went blank
Stiff as a board	Moved in slow motion
White as a ghost	Felt like being stuck in quick sand
Chattering teeth	Everything closing in
Lump in my throat	Felt heavy
In a daze	Hyperventilated
Braced myself	Head in the clouds
Grit my teeth	Shocked
Keep a stiff upper lip	

---

in the belief: "I can." Positive thinking self-talk adjusts according to the challenge at hand:

- At sporting events: "I can put the ball where I want it to go, because I practice."
- In the classroom: "I can pass this test easily, because I study."
- At home: "I can make mom meals while she's sick, because I help her cook."
- In a violent situation: "I can save myself for the love of my family, because I know how to protect myself."

You don't need to be a motivational speaker to know that people who think positively have more positive outcomes than negative-thinking people because positive thinkers refuse to quit. If challenged, your children's disciplined and practiced determination rooted in "I can" self-talk will be critical for their self-control, crime prevention, and crime survival.

Besides practicing "I can" self-talk (and replacing "I can't" with "I'll try" self-talk) you and your children are encouraged to visualize a special memory or family photo that you want to "scan" into your heart for motivation and positive thinking in a crisis. Just like learning to ride a bike or a skateboard, repeat the ritual of thinking "I can" while seeing this specific photo in your mind on command.

In our home, we all have chosen to visualize a formal family portrait hanging over our fireplace. We fondly call it "the picture." Our daughter recently used it when she was rear-ended by a drunk driver, causing a multicar auto accident:

I was furious until I started to belly-breathe, gripped the handle on my key chain, and imagined "the picture" in my mind. It stabilized me as I decided "I can handle this." While waiting for the police, I wrote down what I could remember.

Through conscious repetition, you and your children will be able to call upon positive thoughts—"I can" self-talk reinforced by pictures of loved ones—for inspiration and self-control in a crisis.

Life Review: The Why of Surviving

We researched survivors of critical incidents (fires, plane crashes, shipwrecks, auto accidents, crimes) to study how they hung on despite overwhelming odds, only to have our belief reinforced that it wasn't *how* they held-on, but *why* they held on. Survivors often are quoted using the cliché: "My life passed before me (like a movie) during the ordeal." Not satisfied with that response, we asked, "What specifically did you see?" Responses are all the same. It wasn't scenes of themselves or specific things in their lives (trophies, cars, places); instead, it was those they loved—mom, dad, son, daughter, sister, brother, and so on. The more we research survival, the more we are convinced that the power of love is the greatest positive force on earth!

Modeling Self-Control

Our kids love to hear stories about our fear and what we did specifically to survive. We have told our kids countless times that we belly-breathed, gripped, and visualized them to get through a crisis. We conduct these short, heartfelt discussions with our children the minute we walk in the door because they provide a chance to review courage and the three inner actions we want them to model for self-control. Our most recent disclosure was driving through foggy West Virginia mountains during an ice storm, in the middle of the night:

Our extreme belly-breathing for three straight hours while driving in the mountains totally fogged up the inside of our windshield. Constant blowing of the defroster on "high" caused our lips to chap. Dad's hands felt like he had arthritis from gripping the steering wheel tightly while fighting 50 mph winds. Mom had a tight hold on a pillow, looking for stray deer rushing out of the woods. And of course, we kept visualizing you (the picture) saying, "We can do this" because there was no way we were going to miss your game tonight. In a similar situation, we know you will do the same thing.

When our children were old enough, we took the power of love to the next level. We've said a few times, "In a worst-case scenario, if we are challenged beyond our ability to survive, feel peace knowing our last thoughts were of you." We feel this brief and positive reference to death is necessary to subtly remind our kids that life is precious, uncertain, frail, and sometimes risky. If you're comfortable doing so, consider making a similar comment to your mature children. This level of honesty will serve as a gigantic booster-shot for their courage. As your

---

Courage Quote

If you face just one opponent

And doubt yourself

You are already outnumbered.

—Dan Millman

children's Courage Coach, you will find that *brief,* heartfelt conversations like this will greatly strengthen your parent-child relationships.

The Quick Guide for Teaching B—Breathe for Self-Control

Fear causes changes inside the body that can shut your children down. To regain control, your children need to know how to engage in three inner actions. You can teach your children these actions using precise action words:

1. Breathe from the belly
2. Grip hands or objects
3. Think positive (visualize loved ones)

4

CRIME PREVENTION: *S* OF BST

From birth to adulthood, your children will cross paths with thousands of strangers. Teaching children to be afraid of all strangers is ridiculous and impractical. What you and your children need are the skills to pick out and control that one-in-a-million threat, whether a stranger or known person, who pretends to be golden but is actually a creep or criminal. This chapter will teach your children to protect their personal space, to listen to their bodies' natural warning system, and to apply color-specific skills for stopping a threat—all keys for helping them protect themselves when the situation is that one-in-a-million threat.

Space Protection

A critical lesson for Courage Coaches to teach their children: "You have the right to protect your body at all times, and you have the right to defend your personal space." Why? Because children cannot be harmed until someone crosses into their personal space. In this chapter, you are going to learn how to teach your children how to keep untrustworthy people out of their space with words and actions. The letter S of our BST Family Defense summarizes space protection.

Hula-Hoop Safety

You can easily demonstrate the concept of personal space protection to your children with one simple tool: a hula-hoop. Memory is enhanced when you use clever props, and a hula-hoop makes the invisible line of elbow-room protection real.

Explain to your children that trustworthy people will never make them uncomfortable by crossing into hula-hoop space. Untrustworthy people disrespect hula-hoop space and force unwanted closeness. Unwanted closeness causes discomfort and fear. Kids often say, "He's a creep" or "She makes me feel creepy." What a great and accurate word! We told our kids that "creeps" are people who are not criminals yet. When creepy people get too close, the oxygen and blood creep rapidly toward the center of a person's body.

Teach your children this core belief: "No one has the right to invade your hula-hoop space without your permission. This includes people you know a lot or a little, especially strangers." For example, "It is OK to allow Grandpa inside your hula-hoop space to hug you. However, if Uncle _____ gives you the creeps, you are allowed to refuse a hug and move away. Keep him out of your hula-hoop space and come find me."

Courage Coaches need to honor their children's reports of creeps and creepy feelings. Those feelings do not need to be logical. Teach your children to consider those changes they feel inside their body as warnings of danger. Explain that sometimes your body feels what your eyes can't yet see or your brain understand. Dogs demonstrate this all the time. If you have a pet dog, observe and discuss how your dog intuitively knows the difference when a family member or stranger comes to the front door. It's something dogs feel before they see. Dogs experience the creeps (labored breathing, heart pounding), sometimes caused by strangers and sometimes caused by people they know and don't like. A creepy feeling is a lifesaving, natural alarm for dogs and for people.

Adjusting Personal Space

Teach your children that although usual personal space protection is the size of a hula-hoop, sometimes personal space is smaller, and sometimes it's larger. To demonstrate this, open the hula-hoop up by the seam, demonstrating smaller by tightly wrapping the hula-hoop around you, and demonstrating larger by excessively opening up the hula-hoop beyond its ends. Explain size changes in hula-hoop space protection this way:

Your normal personal space is about the size of this hula-hoop around you. There will be times you choose to voluntarily get close to people by giving up some of your personal space, like when you wait in food lines at fast food restaurants or crowded school or sporting events. In those cases, the crowd keeps you safe. When playing in our backyard, you are entitled to even larger personal space—our whole backyard. It is unreasonable for anyone— especially strangers—to step one foot inside our backyard without our invitation. If this happens, it will feel wrong, because it is wrong. Breathe and run into the house.

Setups Used for Space Invasion

There are three basic setups used by creeps or criminals to invade your child's personal space. They are created by conversation (or luring), following, or hiding. Response to each setup requires your child to demonstrate courage, self-control, and space protection using effective verbal skills. In this chapter we'll focus on teaching the setups and responses. In upcoming chapters, we'll offer age-appropriate ideas for helping your child practice these self-control and space protection skills.

The Conversation Setup and Self-Protection Response

The Setup

The most frequent setup used when luring a child is the conversation approach because it offers creeps or criminals a safe opportunity to test a child without committing to an attack—yet! They are trying to determine whether the child will be an easy or difficult target. Their phony conversations are actually opportunities to rapidly conduct an interview that shows the child's nervousness or courage, shyness (demonstrated by poor eye contact and a weak voice) or confidence (demonstrated by solid eye contact and a strong voice). In addition, pretending to play while engaging in phony conversations allows them to move into a child's personal space and remain inches from her body, without causing alarm to the child. At any time during a conversation setup, if the criminal becomes fearful of approaching witnesses, he can walk away from a child and not be arrested because, technically, no crimes were committed, just (inappropriate) conversations.

Conversation setups usually start with creeps or criminals asking simple, unthreatening questions like:

"Do you know where _____ is?"
"Will you help me find my lost dog?"
"What time is it?"
"You are so pretty. Would you like to be a model?"
"Are you _____? Your mom is sick and sent me to pick you up."

Creeps or criminals are hoping golden children will remain stuck in helpful, nice mode, and they'll try to distract a child in three different ways:

- *Mind distraction:* They want a child to think about answering questions, rather than think about the bad feelings caused by her inner fear alarm.
- *Hand distraction:* They want a child's hands busy—pointing out directions, reaching into a pocket/purse/school bag for requested item(s), or playing with a toy/object.
- *Eye distraction:* They'll trick a child to innocently look away while pointing out directions, searching for item(s) in pocket/purse/school bag, or playing with an item held in her hand.

A creep who escalates to criminal behavior waits until his three-point distraction is complete, then moves in quickly when the child looks away.

The moment he moves through personal space and grabs the child, he assumes the child will be immobilized by holding her own breath, which strips her of the ability to scream, run, or fight during those first critical seconds.

The Self-Protection Response
To stop conversation setups, teach your child that when a person they know or don't know approaches them to talk, causing creepy feelings even though

the person is being nice, they are allowed to switch to orange. They are allowed to display immediate confidence and courage by rapidly packaging all these responses together for a powerful first impression of strength:

- Belly-breathe, grip hands, and visualize your family.
  This starts to activate your child's self-control.
- Make direct eye contact and hold it.
  Holding eye contact shows your child's confidence and courage. It is rare in children and shows emotional strength that creeps do not want to see in potential victims.
- Say, "I don't know. Go away," or any negative words that stop the conversation.
  Teach your child that it is OK to act mean and speak orange when approached by a creep. Discuss the need to lie on these occasions, and assure your child that she never needs to feel pressured to help creepy people in any way. If they need help, they can get it from someone else—an adult.
- Step back to immediately increase your hula-hoop space.
  Increasing space moves your child out of the creep's immediate reach, preventing a quick grab. It is another statement of confidence and self-control that creeps do not want to see.

What If?

Once your child has mastered the basics, play "What if?" to discuss a creep or criminal's possible reactions to your child's orange response to unwanted closeness.

Question: What if the creep was actually a nice golden person who just walked away?

Answer: Nice people will respect your right to say "no" by walking away. If needy, this person can get help from someone else, preferably an adult. Feel no guilt! It is always better to make safe choices, trusting your inner feelings of danger rather than trusting a person who creates creepy feelings. Remember, when you defend yourself verbally, you are directly and honorably defending our entire family.

Question: What if the creep ignores my "no," keeps talking, and steps forward into my hula-hoop space again?

Answer: Act orange/red, responding to your body's inner warnings of escalating danger (rapid heartbeats and shallow breathing). The creep or criminal is using his power in an attempt to control and intimidate you. Repeat and escalate your performance with more intensity.

- Continue to belly-breathe, grip, and visualize loved ones.
- Escalate to "mean" solid eye contact.
- Firmly repeat "NO!" or any negative statement.
- Step back again, and increase your hula-hoop space.

Encourage your child to add this step:

- While talking, point your finger (like a gun—index finger out, thumb up, bottom fingers back) to show force and identify your invisible space line. This powerful hand motion sends a message, "I am dangerous. Do not cross into my space!" It's possible you and your child have already used this powerful hand motion successfully to scare back a stray dog.

Question: What if the creep gets really angry (red), continues to ignore my "no's," yells at me, and comes into my space again?

Answer: If he is red, you must act red immediately for family defense: Roar and run!

We recommend you teach your children to roar, not scream, when frightened. A scream is a high-pitched shrill sound generated from the neck and chest area. A roar is a deep, intense groan or air release from the stomach area. Most golden children struggle to scream in a crisis because there is no air in their chest and neck. To illustrate this, remind your children of a time when they were winded from a fall or hard hit while playing sports.

Roaring has many benefits. The sound of a roar is likely to draw the attention of witnesses because it sounds distinctly different from a scream and is more easily interpreted as a cry for help—rather than kids playing around. The release of a roar can create red intensity, verbally and physically—startling an attacker and possibly stopping the attack. Finally, roars make your children physically strong.

Running is always a recommended option any time your child feels fear, encounters a creep, or feels danger escalating. It's important for Courage Coaches to understand, however, that running is not always possible. Sometimes there are no places/people/lights to run toward, physical barriers prevent running (e.g., trapped in a room or basement),

"Roar Out the Pain" Practice

Show your children the prevalence of deliberate roaring in sports—of all sorts—when extra power and strength are needed. Watch sporting events together and listen to multimillion-dollar athletes. They never scream for power—they roar for power! Explain that the reason roaring increases physical strength is because it tightens all your muscles. Those tight muscles then serve as a "protective wall" that helps protect you from being winded (by falling or force) in a fight. This is why kids who study karate roar when they are struck by kicks and punches sparring and also when they prepare themselves to break bricks and boards in demonstrations. Convince your children that they have already practiced the power of roaring—when they released that strange sound moving something heavy.

Reprogram your children to roar rather than scream whenever they are suddenly attacked in nonviolent, fearful tests. This new habit is great fun and wonderful practice for the whole family.

Paper cut on your finger?	ROAR out your pain
Finger slammed in a door?	ROAR out your pain
Slip and fall to the ground?	ROAR out your pain
Winded by ball in the stomach?	ROAR out your pain
Face too deep in a hot oven?	ROAR out your pain
Startled by a scary movie?	ROAR out your fear
Find a million dollar lottery ticket?	ROAR and celebrate!

This conscious practice can imprint your children's subconscious mind with a new and much more effective automatic response to breath-stealing fear.

or escalating danger is not apparent—denying the chance to run. Your child needs all the BST Family Defense tools to survive challenges when running is not possible.

Question: What if I can't run?

Answer: If you are trapped, he wants either your things or you.

- Give up things immediately. Think like a bank! Give up money rather than put lives in danger.
- Fight physically for you. Activate BST Family Defense. When he tries to attack you, he is attacking our whole family through your

skin. Do not hesitate. Immediately defend us by defending yourself. (We'll present some easy-to-master and effective physical defense techniques in Chapter 5.)

The Following Setup and Self-Protection Response

The Setup
A creep or criminal watches your child from a distance, then starts to follow—getting close quickly. He is watching for and testing these fear responses:

- Tunnel vision, eyes locked forward
- Arms hanging down, no motion
- Shuffling of the feet rather than a confident walk
- Unwillingness to look around, responding to fear or sounds

The Self-Protection Response
To stop a following setup, teach your children that when a person appears quickly around them (or strange noises occur), especially when they are alone, immediately act orange to display confidence and courage by packaging all these responses together:

- Belly-breathe, grip your hands, and visualize your family.
  This activates your child's self-control.
- Look back by turning your head constantly.
  The last things a creep or criminal wants are his face to be seen repeatedly, and his element of surprise/control to be ruined by a child who confronts fear.
- Make glancing orange eye contact each time your head turns.
  Your child's courageous ability to confront a creep with determined (orange) eye contact sends a powerful, silent message: "I know you are following me. I'm not afraid. Get away!"

What If?
Again, play "What if?" to discuss a creep or criminal's possible reactions to your child's orange response to uncomfortable, rapid closeness. Encourage your child to switch to orange-red or red behavior in response to a creep's escalating danger.

Question: What if the creep quickly moves away because he is a nice golden person (your neighbor jogging) and my rudeness hurt his feelings?

Answer: Adults understand that kids need to be alert and defensive, especially when walking alone. Obviously, our neighbor was impressed with your courage and expression of strength because your actions adjusted his behavior. Odds are, he hopes his own kids can turn on a ferocious (orange) switch like you did in response to a rapidly approaching stranger. You had no way of knowing it was a neighbor, until he was too close. If you want, we can go visit him and talk about it. Honestly, an apology is not necessary. You were tested, and your courageous response was awesome!

Question: What if the creep continues to move toward me, ignoring my strong eye contact and confidence?

Answer: If a creep or criminal ignores your signs of courage while continuing to move rapidly toward you, be ready to move. Your body will keep on warning you with rapid heartbeats and shallow breathing. There is no reason for him to close in on your personal space, except to cause crime. Immediately act orange-red for family defense by running toward lights, people, or buildings for safety, and roar!

Question: What if I can't run?

Answer: Be clever if you can't run. The creep or criminal assumes you will keep moving forward in a predictable path. Besides continuing your brave orange-red choices, especially the glancing eye contact, confuse him with the unexpected. Abruptly change your path:

- Cross the street to change sides.
- Zigzag through parked cars in a lot or on the street.
- Walk around bushes, poles, trash cans, paper racks, trees, etc.
- Cut through moving traffic *safely*.
- *Safely* walk into moving traffic and stand on the middle line.

These unexpected behaviors will confuse the creep or criminal, draw the attention of possible witnesses (especially the ones driving cars), and keep a physical barrier between you and the creep. Your consistent courage, along with confusion caused by abrupt path changes, will force the creep or criminal to make a snap decision: stop or continue.

Question: What if he doesn't stop? What if a creep follows my crazy path around parked cars, and I find myself accidentally trapped?

Answer: If trapped by a creep or criminal with no place to run and no one around to help you, switch to red. Deliver a stunning theatrical performance:

- Stop and turn. Rapidly face him before he is too close. Try to have a minimum of one car length of space between you and the creep or criminal.
- Stare him down with intense red eye contact. This creep is not going to hurt our family through you.
- Point your finger (like a gun).
- Curse! Use red words to stun him. Your goal is to shock the creep with red behavior and words he does not expect. Although we do not speak red words in our home, you are allowed to use them to save your life.

This explosion of red family defense will energize every cell in your child's body. Like a mother bear protecting her cub or the family pet confronted with a stranger, your child is visually and verbally warning a creep to stay away or risk a fight. And those are the choices. The creep either stops, stunned by the red performance, or he continues rushing toward your child's space, forcing your child to physical action—to fight and defend her family by defending herself.

A Note about Vulgarity

Give permission to your children to use red stunning words, without hesitation, in red crime scenarios to stop a pending criminal. Unexpected use of red words by golden children not only stuns creeps—it also stuns golden children to switch into fighter mode. If your child is followed by an unstoppable red creep or criminal, golden words ("Please sir, go away from me, thank you very much") won't stop him. The fastest way for your child to destroy her sweet, kind, and naïve (golden) image in dangerous situations is to be an actress who can quickly color-code her language to match the color of her threat.

Except for crime survival scenarios, create zero tolerance of red words in your home so that your children are clear about their limited and, therefore, powerful effect. Vulgarity, believe it or not, is an effective tool for peace when used to stop violent crime.

The Sudden Setup and Self-Protection Response

The Setup

A creep or criminal targets your child, hides, then moves in quickly or jumps out to startle and grab your child. This is the most dangerous style of attack because your child is at a serious disadvantage—his head, hands, and feet are stripped of their necessary flow of oxygen and blood. These inner changes severely restrict your child's ability to react quickly.

The Self-Protection Response

To survive a sudden setup (because stopping it or preventing it is all but impossible), teach your child that breathing is his first challenge, and the creep touching or grabbing him is actually his second challenge. Explain that the terror of a sudden attack feels like being held under water. Your child needs to struggle wildly (flap around his body and limbs with whatever limited motion he can create)—determined to do whatever it takes to release the air trapped in his belly or stomach. As your child's Courage Coach, give him the words he needs:

- Roar to release air stuck in the lower belly.
- Physically fight. Immediately defend us—by immediately defending yourself.

Crime Prevention

As explained in these three setups used by creeps or criminals, the best way to win a fight is fight avoidance. It's called crime prevention. Your children's self-control and clever space protection skills will be tested many times in their childhood. Sometimes they will know they've been tested. Sometimes, due to their perceived strength, they will not know they've been tested because they scared a creep or criminal away.

Crime prevention cannot be measured. Most of the time, your children's brilliant application of courage and crime prevention skills will go unnoticed. Close calls are rarely reported to the police because nothing really happened. That is why Courage Coaches are needed. Besides teaching these effective family defense skills, you need to respond with joyous celebration to your children's acts of courage. Whether the tests were big or small, realize their success was rooted in loving the family, and especially loving you.

Quick Guide to Teaching S—Protect Space for Crime Prevention

Your children have the right to protect their body and their life at all times. No one is allowed to enter their hula-hoop-sized, personal space without their permission. Criminals use three basic setups to get into your children's space. Crime prevention is possible when your children switch to orange or red actions and words.

Conversation Setup

- Belly-breathe, grip, and visualize loved ones.
- Make direct orange eye contact.
- Give a negative reply.
- Step back (pointing finger).
- Roar and run, or fight.

Following Setup

- Belly-breathe, grip, and visualize loved ones.
- Keep turning head to look back.
- Make glancing orange eye contact.
- Change path abruptly.
- Curse! Use red words.
- Roar and run, or fight.

Sudden Setup

- Roar to release stuck air!
- Fight!

5

CRIME SURVIVAL: *T* OF BS*T*

While the first two parts of our safety equation are often effective in deterring an attack, there may be times when your child needs to do more to protect himself. When crimes are not preventable, it is reasonable for mature children to escalate from verbal to physical force to stop a violent attacker.

The good news is that your children do not need to master a long list of physical techniques. Rather, they need to master one technique they believe they can do that works. After our combined years of studying, teaching, and researching self-defense options, we believe that one strike at the throat is the best crime survival choice. The letter T is used to summarize the word *throat* in our BST Family Defense plan.

Changing Colors

Striking the throat is a serious choice with serious consequences that you'll need to share with your children. Upfront, we acknowledge this is going to be a difficult conversation with your kids. That's good. Your discomfort with the subject is a statement that you and your family are golden people who prefer to care, give, and help rather than strike another human being. If the world were filled with people as golden as your family, books like this would not need to be written. However, you are reading this book because you know the world has a small percentage of red personalities who don't care about the safety and well-being of you or your children. Your children need powerful survival beliefs and one physical choice to survive unpreventable crime.

Remind your children that in a violent encounter, they need to switch colors, which is a form of acting. Assure your children they have the right and the need to change their behavior to match the color of their attacker's behavior (red) plus 1 percent.

The Switch

Your children's survival depends on their ability to rapidly switch from being nice and golden, to acting orange for crime prevention, then red for crime survival. If the attacker is red (acting violently) and your children remain golden or escalate only to orange, the attacker has the advantage. To survive violent force, nice kids need to use counterforce for whatever amount of time it takes to stop the attacker and escape. As a Courage Coach, make sure your children understand that using counterforce and acting violent to save their own life does not make them violent people. Your children are golden people forced to take action to protect themselves.

To help reinforce the need for this sudden switch, use a second visual prompt. Touch a light switch on the wall and say, "Just as this room can go from complete darkness to bright light in a split second, you have a switch that allows you to go from being gold through orange and into red in a split second." By connecting this lifesaving attitude to an everyday visible object like a light switch, you are creating a healthy memory trigger.

Passionately teach your children their right to switch colors (behavior). Self-doubt and limited beliefs, such as *Maybe I can, I'm not sure, I might, I can't, or I won't,* are not acceptable self-talk or self-thoughts for effective crime survival. Thoughts create beliefs; beliefs create behavior.

Repeatedly remind your children that when law-abiding citizens (adults and children) use red behavior, their motivation for survival is rooted in love of family, not hatred of the attacker. Further explain that by stopping the violence rapidly, and escaping as soon as possible, they are actively defending you and their entire family from further emotional

---

Never Wait to Fight Back

....

Avoid the term *fight back* when you discuss physical fighting scenarios with your children. It implies tolerance of your child getting hit first—so she can then fight "back." Instead, you want to make sure your child has the advantage by hitting first, not fighting back.

Hitting first does not make your child the aggressor. The attacker coming after your child is the aggressor. Your child is fighting efficiently and defensively by striking an unstoppable criminal first when her personal space is invaded. Your child has the right to defend herself against the threat of violence (once she has a *reasonable* fear that the criminal is going to cause physical harm) and does not have to wait until the *actual* violence occurs. That reasonable fear is hula-hoop space invasion, especially after your child does all in her power to turn orange and red, in action and in words, to defend her space.

---

pain. Reframing your children's motivation to survive for love will reduce any golden hesitation they may have when making life-and-death decisions.

Crime Survival: It's about Air!

In violence, the technical winner is the one who is breathing when the fight is over. Your child's goal is to stop the attacker's airflow before the attacker has the chance to stop your child's airflow by grabbing her nose or mouth, throat, or chest. If the attacker is not breathing, he cannot continue to attack your child, even if he's bigger and stronger.

The Best "Striking Throat" Technique

We believe effective crime survival requires the repetition of internal practice (permission statements, mental rehearsals, righteous beliefs, and so on)

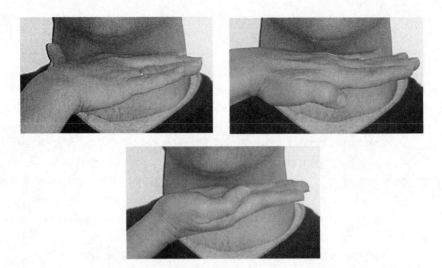

Figure 5.1 To effectively stop an attacker's air, teach your child to strike the throat with an opened, flat hand rather than a punch or a fist. The hand can be in any one of these three positions.

more so than external (physical) practice. Helping your children develop and master multiple defensive techniques is not your goal. As their Courage Coach, you need to emphasize to your children the one most important technique in a red physical attack—striking the attacker's throat while defending their own.

Instruct your children to strike the throat with an opened flat hand rather than a punch or a fist. Either edge of your children's flattened hands creates the best, most effective weapon (See Figure 5.1).

Use a cup and saucer for a visual demonstration. Show your children how a cup is about the same width and height of a closed fist, and a saucer is narrow like an opened, flat hand. Using your own throat, gently show your children how the edge of a flat saucer rather than the side of a cup would cause the quickest and most efficient damage to a person's throat. Again, the more you can connect lifesaving lessons to clever everyday visuals, the deeper you create lasting, lifesaving memories.

Note: Make sure your children know that they are *never* allowed to practice this technique on another person. Red behavior has

---

"Love" Hands

When our son was 10 years old, he made a great observation and recommendation after watching our seminar. Instead of using the word *slice* to describe striking the throat, Jimmy suggested we teach "Hit with love" demonstrating that my hand position actually looks like the letter L when I demonstrated the strike the throat technique.

The thumb-side of a hand looks like a capital L when the thumb sticks out. The backside of a hand looks like a lowercase I when a hand is tight.

Take this concept to the next level. When you leave your children, always wave good-bye using your love hand position (which looks a lot like a high five). Use this common hand motion to mean more than just good-bye. Use it as a tool to regularly remind your children of their rights and natural power every time they leave your side.

---

dramatic consequences, and while practicing on objects is OK, using the throat strike on another person is unacceptable, unless that person is a criminal. You know your child better than anyone else, and if your child is fascinated by violence or doesn't display a sense of maturity when discussing crime survival, you should carefully decide when it's appropriate to introduce this technique.

HOMEWORK ASSIGNMENT

The human throat is a very frail organ. Like the cardboard tube that supports a roll of paper towels, the walls of the human throat collapse easily when struck.

Encourage your children to practice striking the throat by hitting cardboard paper towel tubes or toilet paper tubes. Hold the tube in the center of one hand as your child strikes it using the "L of Love" with their other hand (See Figure 5.2). Encourage him to roar out an exhale from deep in his belly as he strikes the tube. Such a blow can effectively stop an attacker, as he struggles to regain air, giving your child vital seconds or, hopefully, minutes to escape.

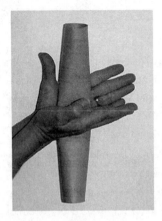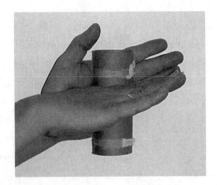

Figure 5.2 Using paper towel tubes and toilet paper tubes, practice the motions needed to make an effective throat strike.

What If?

When Courage Coaches discuss how to physically fight red attackers, it is likely that children will have many "What If?" questions.

Question: What if I can't reach his throat because I am short?

Answer: A large/tall attacker must bend down to your level to grab you or pick you up. When the attacker lowers his body—especially his throat—in an effort to touch you, that is your chance to use the additional length of your outstretched arm to strike the attacker's throat first!

Question: What if I am not strong enough? How hard do I hit?

Answer: Very little force is needed to interrupt oxygen flowing in a throat. The human throat is a frail organ, not protected by bone or muscle. It is vulnerable to serious injury when struck with anything, especially narrow objects like your flat Love hand. If you can throw a ball, you can interrupt an attacker's airflow easily. The collapse of the throat tube is very similar to what you feel when you strike the paper towel tubes. **Because it is so easy, and the injury is so severe, you may *never* practice on anyone.** Striking the throat works! Therefore, it only can be practiced on cardboard tubes.

Question: What if my hand is stuck in an odd position under the attacker's neck and I can't move it enough to hit with a "slice" motion?

Success Story!

. . . .

Years ago, a young high school teacher called to relay a touching Christmas "Empowerment Story" that occurred in her family.

Months before, the young teacher survived a brutal rape by a man who suddenly jumped out at her as she was locking the front door of the school after an evening music event. Weeks later, the high school sponsored our evening seminar in celebration of the teacher's courage and survival.

After the holidays, this brave survivor called to describe an event that occurred while opening Christmas presents with her family. Her 12-year-old sister—who had attended our seminar with the survivor's entire family— insisted that their mother open her "very special, large present first." The entire family was anxious to see what was in the surprise package that made the little sister so proud.

As the mother opened the gift, she gently started to cry as she read a note that accompanied a department store box filled with dozens of crushed cardboard paper towel tubes.

The note read...

Mom, I just want you to know ... I AM READY.
I love you...

Continuing the story, the teacher reported her whole family broke down and cried as the meaning behind the gift of crushed paper towel tubes became evident. The Christmas gift was a symbol of courage, love, and preparedness that no one will forget, especially the empowered 12-year-old sister.

Answer: Besides a flat-hand strike to the throat, you can grab and crush an attacker's throat tube (a motion much like crushing a soda can). A firm crush of the throat can cause an attacker serious injury and even death. When you are trapped in a life-or-death scenario, do whatever you can, any way you can, to save your life. Remember, you are defending us when you defend yourself.

Question: What if I'm holding something in my hands?

Answer: Drop it. However, if the item is somewhat narrow (a cell phone, highlighter/marker/pen, keys, small book/notebook, comb/brush end), use it as a weapon to strike the throat. An advantage of having an item in your hand(s) is that the grip/squeeze you have on that item automatically circulates your blood and oxygen, helping you prepare to fight. A second advantage of a narrow item in your hand is that you will likely hit faster, because you do not have to actually touch the attacker's skin/throat.

Question: What if I'm knocked to the ground? Should I at least try to kick the groin?

Answer: Do whatever it takes to keep an attacker off of you. Remember that striking the groin only hurts men who feel pain. If your attacker does not feel because of an excessive amount of drugs and/or alcohol in his system, kicks to the groin alone may not stop him. You need to keep struggling until you can strike the attacker's throat, which *will* stop him.

Question: What if he has a big nose? Should I hit his nose or poke his eyes?

Answer: A strike to the eyes and nose can cause incapacitating injury if it is delivered with extreme force. The problem is, it may be hard to hit someone's eyes or smash a nose because those choices require conquering the discomfort of the criminal's body fluid touching your hands. It is much easier physically and emotionally to stop an attacker by striking the throat.

K.I.S.S.: Keep It Simple, Survivor!

There are two additional reasons why we believe teaching your children to strike the throat is the single best defensive tactic to believe in and practice (on paper tubes only).

1. How many animals fight for their life by attacking their opponents' groin? Eyes? Nose? None! How many animals save their own lives by going for their opponent's throat? Many!
2. In first-aid courses, lifesaving choices are taught to be performed in this A–B–C order of importance at a rescue.
   Check the **A**ir
   Check the **B**leeding
   Check **C**irculation

Emphasize to your children that when it comes to survival of any kind, air is the most critical function!

Quick Guide to *T:* Crime Survival

Rarely will your children be forced to physically fight in order to stop an attacker. In preparation for that moment, teach your mature children how to effectively disable an attacker with one quick stroke to the throat.

- Strike the criminal's throat with an opened, flat hand.
- Strike first.
- Strike to cause injury, not just pain.
- Never practice on people, only on cardboard tubes.

Teach and Review the BST Message

Now that you're familiar with all the steps of the BST message, make it part of daily discussions. Using stories in the news, role-play with your children, engaging them in short reminder conversations about what they would do, always using a tone that shows your confidence in them: "You are a courageous kid; what would *you* do?" Depending on the details of the news story and age-appropriateness of each child, listen carefully for your children's selection of words and actions to reflect the proper application of these BST foundation truths. Work to get variations of the following responses, and review them with your children if necessary:

- I would first belly-breathe, grip something or my hands, and think of my family to get myself together.
- If possible, I would run to escape. If trapped or tricked, I know it is not my fault. I will find a way, even if it means fighting, to come home.
- If someone creates unwanted closeness, crossing into my hula-hoop personal space, I will step back to reclaim my space, act orange, and scare the creep away with loud verbal commands. To prevent

crime, I know I am allowed to lie, curse, and roar. Probably, I'll say something like: "Stop! Get away from me. Get the (vulgarity) away from me!"

- If trapped, I know I have the right to physically fight to defend my body and my life at all times! I won't fight for my things—they can be replaced—I will just fight for me.

- I know a police officer or adult is not likely to appear to save me or tell me what to do (give permission to escalate). My safety is my responsibility and I'll figure out what to do by listening and trusting my inside warnings (oxygen and blood shifts). What I see and what I feel will be my guide to switch to orange and red actions.

- If I cannot run or stop the attacker by moving my space and using red words, and there are no other options, I will hit first—the exact second my invisible space (line) is invaded by the criminal trying to grab me. The element of surprise is on my side because an attacker is likely to assume I'll stay golden and terrified, instead of red and courageous!

- I will not allow the criminal to grab me first and touch my air. In red violence, I know his goal is to stop my breathing so I can't move or make noise. I will absolutely not allow him to cover my mouth, pinch my nose shut, hit my throat, or crush my chest. I will take away his air before he gets mine!

Yes, They Can!

Can you imagine your children armed with these passionate, powerful beliefs? Can you imagine them accurately sharing those beliefs with you every time you discuss personal safety? Is this level of empowerment really possible for children to learn and believe throughout their childhood?

Absolutely! We know. We have two such believers in our home! We are not bragging; instead, we want you to know it's possible to raise children who can protect themselves. Your children can handle it. In fact, they will thrive knowing how to protect themselves. Courage lessons from you will straighten their backbone and release unnecessary childhood fears. Most important of all, the gift of teaching real-world red will let them know how much you trust them.

- I will strike the criminal with the intention to cause injury ... not just pain. I know I need to stop him so I can run away. If he doesn't stop when I turn orange, I have no choice but to make my first hit and cause injury.
- I will hit the throat and run. I want him to cough/choke so I can get away. When he can't breathe, he can't hurt me. If I miss the throat, I will try again and again until I get it. If needed, I'll kick and struggle any way I can, until I get his throat.

Part 3 offers age-specific ideas for developing courage and healthy safety practices (rooted in our BST Family Defense plan). Regardless of your child's age, we recommend that you read every chapter because most ideas can be applied, with slight adjustments, at any age.

PART 3

SELF-PROTECTION
TECHNIQUES

6

SIGNS AND SYMBOLS
OF COURAGE STARTING AT
AGE 3 AND UP

B y the time your children are 3 years old, we suggest you start teaching them a strong, clear plan that honors their natural feelings and
gives them an introduction to personal power and decision-making.
Three is an age when most children can comprehend cause–and–effect
concepts (as in, if you put your toys away in the toy box, you can have
a cookie). Look forward to practicing small acts of courage and safety
that will also enhance development of your children's self-control, personal discipline, and courage during ages 3, 4, and 5.

Yes, You Can!

We are convinced that scared children are not safer children. Instead, we
believe confident, disciplined children are safer children. When you start
to teach concepts of self-protection and courage to your young children,
do all in your power to teach with electrifying energy rooted in the power
of love and with an "of course you can do it" spirit. Your young children
need you to talk about safety with a tone opposite the one most likely used
by your parents. We know it's hard because like your parents, you are
deathly afraid of your child being harmed. It takes great discipline for
Courage Coaches to hide that constant concern in order to present a solid
image of confidence, but isn't that what coaches do—accept the worst and

prepare for the best? Smile and speak with great enthusiasm. How you talk to your young children about crime is almost as important as what you say.

In this chapter, you'll learn how to give your children a courage and safety vocabulary, one that they'll be able to draw upon when you're not there to protect them. You'll find ways to make discussions on courage and personal safety one of your children's favorite topics. Not only will they remember it and feel confident themselves, they'll be drawing on the power of positive family interaction while learning the building blocks to the BST Family Defense plan.

Label Makers

Your own verbal discipline is critically important when communicating with your children. It takes discipline to filter what comes out of your mouth when you are upset or scared. As parents, you need to remember that children will take your labels to heart, good or bad. We

---

Mr. Safety

When our son was little, we called him Mr. Safety. Even today he continues to have a keen eye for anticipating things that are about to fall, burn, hurt, or injure. Without being annoying, he has become a master at verbally or physically correcting near-misses, such as moving a pot handle away from a stove's edge or picking up stray items on the steps. Besides the compliments, he's also enjoyed the occasional power it gives him since he's stuck being the youngest in the family.

Jimmy's skill for anticipating danger and making adjustments gave us a genuine sense of comfort and trust as he grew up playing contact sports, boating, jet skiing, and even competitively racing go-carts (as fast as 90 mph). Is his keen sensitivity toward danger and willingness to make quick corrections a natural or learned habit? We believe it is a learned habit due to years of deliberate positive reinforcement. Jimmy believes his nickname is a positive label, and he values the consistent (not exaggerated) celebration of his keen safety insights and courage.

encourage you to look for positive labels that will compliment and deliberately empower your child—nicknames that can be conveyed with sincerity, for example, Mr. Safety, Ms. Detective, Mr. Dependable, Courage Kid, Ms. Positive, Mr. Amazing, and so on.

Your children will live up or down to your expectations, your belief in their ability, and the lifetime labels you assign. Be diligent and watch your children carefully when they are young. Look for their positive unique factor and translate it to applications of safety and courage.

Confidence-Building Tasks

To encourage courage and self-sufficiency, acknowledge your children for their strengths and positive beliefs while they perform tasks around the house. Ask your young child to help you open jars (after you secretly loosened the lid).

Joey, you're such a strong little boy. Thanks for helping me. You can do just about anything because you are willing to try.

These small acts of contribution make your children feel like important members of your family team. The sincere sense of belonging and helping is important for young children. Helping around the house means parents need to slow down, give instructions, and possibly correct a less-than-perfect attempt. However, helping also develops confidence. Confidence in a crisis is the by-product of a priceless foundation of family trust and the ultimate development of self-trust.

Courage-Building Models

As you cultivate your child's confidence, be on the lookout for opportunities to turn everyday events into safety and courage-building lessons. You'll be surprised at the opportunities you can find in daily activities: watching television or movies, playing games, eating out, doing school projects, and talking at the dinner table. For example, you may discuss how the firefighter just seen on the news was able to save an elderly lady because he was belly-breathing, gripping (the lady), and thinking, "I can do this!" Talk about the honor a child brought to his family when he returned a lost wallet. Really get excited when there is a news account about a small child who was able to dial 9-1-1 for a family member in need. Say to your child, "WOW, what courage! I know you can do that too!"

Be careful to not slip into a lecture. Quick one-line lessons are all young children want to hear. Do all in your power to be clever finding courage models and positive examples as you work hard to avoid the dreaded and terrifying "safety talks."

Stories and storytelling can be powerful courage models for children. Make it a family ritual to read your kids bedtime stories that inspire them. *The Little Engine That Could* is our absolute favorite. Its mantra, "I Think I Can, I Think I Can," is priceless when embedded in your child's memory because it creates positive, hypnotic self-talk for surviving tough times. (You'll find further suggestions for courage-based stories in the Resources section at the end of this book.)

We encourage you to create your own bedtime stories that highlight heroics involving your family members. Talk about Grandpa's years as a soldier or Aunt Katie's days as a nurse for newborn babies. Frame a story around how their actions were selfless and benefited others in a time of crisis. Explain that the reason your family made it through those tough times years ago is because of their personal courage. Then say something like, "Guess what! Just like your inheritance of their brown eyes and high cheekbones, you also have inherited their courage—it's in your blood! Like them, you will always find a way!"

Start Your Kids Early on the Safety Equation

Even though children between the ages of 3 and 5 are too young to learn the *T* of the safety equation, you can begin cultivating the *B* and *S* skills in them at this early age. In the next section, you'll find simple and effective ways to begin teaching your children the importance of controlled breathing and space awareness, skills that will help them if they're ever in a compromising situation.

Belly-Breathing for Self-Control

As we discussed in Chapter 3, to regain self-control when frightened, people need to:

- Breathe
- Grip their hand(s) or an object
- Focus on loved ones and positive thoughts

This is true for young children too! Observe your children carefully when they play. Notice how they can easily create shrill screams, using air from their throat and chest (not their belly). Children mostly breathe and talk with shallow breaths from their chest. When extremely afraid or upset, children quickly lose control of that shallow airflow.

When your children are afraid or upset, repeat these specific instructions for their emotional recovery and self-control:

1. *"Breathe deeply."* (You must move air up from your belly.)
2. *"Grip your hands."* (This will move blood from your pounding heart.)
3. *"Mom and Dad are proud of you."* (Describe appropriate positive thoughts, for example, "You'll be home soon." "You're a brave girl/boy.)"

You'll discover that these specific instructions are useful when soothing a child who is facing a medical procedure or an emergency, such as a bee sting, broken arm, booster shots at the doctor, or dog bite. By implementing them whenever your child becomes upset, your child will begin to put them into practice on her own.

If your small child is severely acting out in theatrical hysterics (she is really mad and wants to control you), immediately stop what you are doing. Take her by the hand. Escort her to a quiet place. First, check her breathing. Tell her to match your breathing as you take slow, deep belly-breaths. (Forget about the problem that caused the outburst for now.) Put your hand on her belly and tell her to push your hand out by breathing deeply from her belly. Give her something to hang on to (squeeze) like car keys, a fat pen or marker, or a cell phone. Correcting your child's breathing will slow down, then stop, her hysteria. Once under emotional control, talk quietly and firmly, with strong eye contact as you discuss the problem that created the hysterics.

BOOM! Or Ouch!

Small children are easily frightened by loud noises and darkness. These unexpected conditions can provide many opportunities to practice courage and self-control. Whenever darkness or loud noises stun your children (for example, chair falls, engine backfires, glass breaks or power outage) immediately check for an opportunity to coach them with recovery words: belly-breathe, grip, think positive. Do it yourself, Courage Coach, then guide them to model your recovery response.

Every time your child falls or bumps his head, encourage him to belly-breathe and roar—exhaling deep sounds from his belly. Make quick recovery from breath-holding a routine game in your home. (Your child isn't the only one who is stunned in small accidents: "Yes, honey, I wish daddy would just roar when he hammers his thumb instead of saying that red word.")

When guiding your children through controlling their fear, be careful not to play games or humor your children with false fears like ghosts in the room. Although it may seem harmless when young children interpret odd shadows in their bedrooms as ghosts, the lifetime consequences of validating false fears is costly. I know it takes time; however, it is critical that you calmly walk your child to the place she sees a ghost every time and confront it. While walking, coach her to belly-breathe, grip, and be brave (positive thought). Be sure to compliment her. "It took courage to look, even though we didn't find anything." (Do *not* say, "See, you were wrong.")

Sometimes, young children have learned they can delay their bedtime by creating false monsters and ghosts for attention. The parents respond with a big hug, saying, "Don't worry, I'll protect you," then allow their child to move to a different bedroom or the couch. What the child learns besides delaying bedtime is, "It feels good to hide my eyes, get a big hug and lots of loving attention when I am afraid for real and for fake." Rewarding fear behaviors undermines your goal to teach your child to confront challenges with eye contact. You can still cherish

---

The Postponed Hug

When our daughter was 5, she fell asleep in my bed watching TV with me. Mike was working night shift. Our old furnace made a sudden loud sound that woke Jaclyn up, visibly startling her. She was sure an intruder was in the house. My first impulse was to be a traditional protective mom, comforting Jaclyn with a big bear hug that would bury her eyes in my chest. (I remember thinking that a big hug would feel so good.) Then I stopped. I knew I couldn't teach her to respond to fear by hiding her eyes. Sure, I could be her hero and protector (and get an extended, emotional hug) but at what cost?

This was a teachable moment! Jaclyn needed to be her own hero by confronting and conquering her fear. (Obviously, I knew no intruder was in the house, just an old grumpy furnace.) I grabbed her by the hand (gripping tightly) and encouraged her to belly-breathe as we turned on lights, checking every room and closet. We even checked the entire basement until she was convinced there was no danger in the house. As we walked around, I continually stated how proud Dad was going to be by her demonstration of courage and investigation skills. (In my mind I could see her in her own home someday, mimicking this experience, fighting for and finding the courage to investigate strange sounds while alone at night.)

After double-checking the door locks, we went back to the bedroom because Jaclyn was convinced she was safe. I bent down to give her a huge celebration hug (so her head and eyes were over my shoulder) in honor of her proven bravery and future courage. Instead of me being Jaclyn's hero, she was mine that night.

---

hugs from your child at other times for other reasons without reinforcing weak behavior.

Teaching Space Awareness to Toddlers

As we discussed earlier, hula-hoops provide a tangible way to teach kids the concept of personal space. This works with preschoolers too. As you work with them and a hula-hoop, tell them the following:

1. No one is allowed inside your personal hula-hoop space without your permission.
2. No one is allowed to touch your body without your permission because your body is inside the hula-hoop space.
3. Your body will warn you when untrustworthy people (known and unknown) get too close to your hula-hoop space, and you'll feel the "creeps."

Creeps

You don't want to create fearful children—rather, you want to create children who can withstand fear. Introducing the idea of harmful strangers to your preschooler can be tough and scary, for both you and her. There are simple principles you can put into practice in a loving environment that she can draw upon when needed. Explain to your child that people are a lot like fish that swim with us in the ocean: Most fish will not hurt you, although we always need to respond to the rare feeling of danger caused by the one kind of fish that is dangerous—an approaching shark. Likewise, most people are nice and have no intention of hurting you, although we always need to respond to the feeling of danger caused by an approaching creep.

As we discussed in Chapter 4, using the word *creep* provides an accurate portrayal of what happens inside your children's body when they are afraid. Teach your children that they have an automatic danger alarm inside their body (just like the family dog) that will cause creepy feelings when someone is untrustworthy or getting too close. They need to listen to their inside warnings—and get away—every time (just like your dog honors its inside warnings every time). Specifically describe inside changes caused by creepy feelings as:

- Rapid breathing (demonstrate rapid, shallow breathing)
- Rapid heart pounding (demonstrate by tapping your hand rapidly over your heart)

Tell your kids, "You will always know who the creeps are because magically your body warns you by making your breathing and heart beat fast! Those inside feelings are your body's natural alarm telling you to get away! Sometimes your brain doesn't understand the changes that your body feels. That's OK. Trust your body's natural alarm (intuition) and get away from creeps."

You can also use your kitchen's smoke alarm for a fun, visual metaphor for the feeling of the creeps. Consider this explanation: The alarm goes off in the kitchen when bacon is burning to warn us that dangerous smoke is creeping too close, just like our heart pounds wildly to warn us when creepy people are getting too close! In both cases get away and tell someone.

Watch carefully and observe your children's instinctive response during minor fearful events, then celebrate their recognition of their own creepy feelings, however small:

Honey, I saw you move away from that man in the gas station. He was a bit creepy. You are so brave when you pay attention to bad feelings and move away. I scooted away from him too, following you! I want you to know I always feel safe around you because you are so good at feeling danger and taking control of yourself by breathing, gripping, and moving your space away from possible danger.

This type of observation and communication has many benefits. It:

1. Lets your child know you are watching him carefully
2. Creates a celebration opportunity to honor natural courage in response to bad feelings: a "creep"
3. Allows you to compliment your child for leading you to safety (slight exaggeration is acceptable)
4. Bonus! What your child thinks is a compliment is actually an opportunity to remind him or her of specific self-control tools: "You are so good at breathing, gripping (thinking positive), and moving your space when you feel creepy...."

You need to also share stories about times you, the Courage Coach, felt uneasy and moved away from creeps and creepy situations. Through your stories, explain that sometimes strangers make you feel creepy. Sometimes people you know, a little or a lot, make you feel creepy. Sometimes, a person who was trustworthy in the past can make you feel creepy now. Reemphasize that it is not important to understand "why" you feel creepy, it's just important to listen to your body's warnings and get away:

When I was at the cookout, our neighbor Eric was acting strange. I appreciate that he cuts our grass when we go on vacation. However, when he stood too close to me, telling me dumb jokes, I really got the creeps and just decided to come home. I usually don't feel that way about him. He wasn't doing anything wrong. It just felt wrong. So I left, just like I know you will get away from people who make you feel "creepy."

A Creep in the Checkout Line

I (Mike) testified as an expert witness for the FBI in a murder case when our daughter was 2 years old. Unfortunately, the defendant was found not guilty on a technicality. Several weeks later while at a local department store, I was in the checkout lane, holding our daughter in my arms. The defendant tapped me on the shoulder and said, "Hey, aren't you the Cincinnati cop that testified against me?" I didn't immediately recognize him, but he sure recognized me. The interesting part of this incident is that our daughter displayed extreme anxiety as this "creepy stranger" approached, many seconds before he spoke. Jaclyn had a clear view over my back and attempted to warn me of pending danger by squeezing my neck extra hard as this man approached. I could feel her heart racing. The conversation was obviously brief. On the way to the car, I thanked Jaclyn for being a good "squeezer," which is about all she could comprehend. When she was a little older, Jaclyn enjoyed hearing me brag about her courage and the success of her natural warning system ... at age 2!

Too Many Creeps

You may be wondering, "What if my child gets the creeps from everyone, unnecessarily? How do I teach her to discern when the creeps are valid, and when she's just being rude?" Monitor your children's creep assessment. If you suspect their feelings are based strictly on appearance such as a scar, mole, disfigurement, or are an attention-getting ploy, avoid a lecture about hurtful, unnecessary judgments and become a "model." Demonstrate golden behavior yourself by interacting with that person in a small way (compliment her hat, sweater, purse). Keep hula-hoop space as you approach to talk. Polite conversation with a person who is different while keeping proper distance is a wonderful life-skill to demonstrate. At a later time, ask your child why he felt the creeps about a certain person. Correct or validate his assumptions. Help him to learn how to fairly judge creepiness, reminding him that scary-looking people over *there* are not worthy of a reaction, but scary-looking people over *here,* who create unwanted closeness and space violations, are worthy of a proper reaction to get away.

It's OK to Stop Hugging Creeps

As parents of youngsters learning to trust themselves, you need to be careful not to train the developing instinct of feeling the creeps out of them by forcing them to violate natural instincts in order to hug "creepy people," especially relatives and friends. Instead of an awkward hug, allow your young children the alternative choice of greeting your relatives and friends by just saying, "Hello" with eye contact and possibly a businesslike handshake.

While you want to support your child as he begins to trust his instincts, allowing him to completely ignore a greeting from a relative or friend (by hiding behind you, running away, and so on) is not recommended for two reasons:

1. It *is* rude. Saying hello to your relative or friend while standing at your side is not dangerous for your child.
2. It reinforces unnecessary social bashfulness. The fear of talking with eye contact needs to be conquered in childhood. Saying hello and looking at a parent's relative or friend is excellent practice for building reasonable social skills as well as courage for safety development.

We believe it is reasonable to empower your young children with personal rights that allow them to make adultlike choices such as:

1. Only hug people you want to hug.
2. Only sit near people you want to sit near.

3. No sitting on laps except for quick visits with Santa and ____ (list trusted exceptions such as Mom, Dad, Grandma, Grandpa, and so on).
4. Get away from creeps who move close to your hula-hoop space.

Someone's Crossed the Line ... What Now?

Teach your children specific reactions to hula-hoop invasion.

If a creepy person gets too close to your personal hula-hoop space:

1. Belly-breathe and run toward people and lights.
2. Ask for help from a trusted person. If none are available, ask help from a woman stranger (statistically, women are less likely to be child abusers).
3. Crawl under a *parked* car if you are trapped and/or alone. (Make sure you emphasize *parked* car.) Be a Mighty Mite! Little children fit under cars. Adults don't. If the creep reaches for you, roll away and make noise. Roar and yell, "I don't know you. Go away!"

Hula-Hoop Invaders—Exceptions

Of course there are times when people will need to enter your preschooler's personal space. The key is to talk about these instances with your child, so she knows the only time it's OK is when you are there. Whenever you take your child to the doctor or dentist, explain that you (the parent) are giving the doctors and nurses permission to reach through her hula-hoop space and enter her intimate space in order to touch her body for the physical checkup.

As described in Chapter 4, be sure to visually show your young children that the reasonable amount of their personal hula-hoop space sometimes changes throughout the day. This is important to discuss so they do not overreact in crowded, yet safe environments. For example, they have full hula-hoop space when sitting at their desk in preschool. They have more than hula-hoop space when playing alone in the driveway (because it's your entire yard). But they have less than hula-hoop space when standing in line for food or riding in a crowded elevator at the mall (at which time the crowd helps keep your space).

Junk Food Courage Runs

There are many safe places where even your young children can practice controlled breathing and space protection. By the time your kids are 10 years old, they can be masters of self-control and thoroughly effective in realistic crime prevention tactics. Starting with preschoolers, you can encourage eye contact and strong communication skills by taking your kids on "courage" practice runs.

When eating out, try making "order your own food" a nonnegotiable rule in your family. Ordering food in all restaurants provides great practice; however, ordering in fast food restaurants is the best. By having your children order their own food, you encourage them to speak clearly and loudly to an adult, practice eye contact, and use other courage techniques in a situation that's safe (you're nearby).

When you're at a fast food restaurant and you're ready to order, choose a line with a clerk who seems tired, short-tempered, extremely tall, the opposite race, and/or the opposite sex of your child. And then send your child up to order:

> CHILD: Mom, order me a kiddie meal.
>
> PARENT: No, you are a big boy ... order your kiddie meal yourself.
>
> CHILD: I don't want to! [Child is upset; his breathing is rapid, and his heart is racing, just as it would be if he were really being attacked.]
>
> PARENT: Take a deep belly-breath. Grip your hands. Look the clerk in the eyes. Speak loudly and clearly order your food.
>
> CHILD: [head down, whispering to clerk] I want a kiddie meal with a small coke ...
>
> CLERK: What? [Great! The clerk just scared your child, exactly what you wanted!]
>
> CHILD: [drops head, punches your thigh and whines]: Pleeeassse order for me.
>
> PARENT: No! Breathe deeply, grip your hands, look her in the eyes, and repeat your order loudly and clearly—or you won't eat. [Be firm.]
>
> CHILD [struggles for self-control in order to repeat his food order, but he repeats it loudly and clearly]: I want a kiddie meal with a small coke, please!

Although this is an exciting breakthrough for your family, you may aggravate the clerk because you won't talk for your child in order to make her job easy. That's OK. You created a real-life courage lesson disguised as a meal selection.

After you sit down to eat, congratulate your child's display of courage in ordering his food. Embellish your praise a little with a personal disclosure: "Jason, I am proud of how you just ordered your meal. That is one of the scariest, tallest people I have ever seen. You, however, gained control of yourself and got the job done. You breathed from your belly, gripped your hands, looked her straight in the eyes and ordered your food, not just once, but twice. (Use this opportunity to compliment your child and repeat the self-control procedures.) You're so awesome. Here's a dollar. After you finish your hamburger, you can go get some ice cream or cookies; or put the money in your bank at home."

Your child will be thrilled with your observation of his courage and the subsequent reward. If the choice is ice cream or cookies, encourage your child to walk up to the ordering counter by himself! That way he gets to act brave all over again, and this time you are not at his side for emotional or verbal support.

You can vary this routine by having your child place your custom-cut lunchmeat orders in the deli department. This is awkward and difficult for young children because the deli counters are so high, and they are forced to talk up and over the counter to strangers. Remind your child of the courage tools: belly-breathe, grip your hands, look the clerk in the eyes, and speak clearly. Observe the struggle from a short distance away. Afterward, praise your child verbally (or with the reward of one favorite food selection). Acknowledge that it is difficult for her to be recognized as a customer, to talk over the counter, and remember a complicated deli order: for example, a half pound of ham, sliced thin, 1 pound of medium sliced Swiss cheese. What a brave girl!

Having your child order food is a valuable opportunity for building courage and communication skills. Rest assured that this test is safe because it is done within your sight, just a few feet away from you. (Make it a habit to pick a table close to the cash register area in fast food restaurants.) However, don't test your young children's courage by sending them off to a restaurant (public) bathroom alone because when the door shuts, your view is blinded and their safety cannot be monitored.

When you allow your children to experience the creeps (shifting oxygen and blood flow) and struggle for self-control in as many safe scenarios as possible, you prepare them in case they ever experience real danger. If your child needs to be brave for real, make sure it isn't the first time.

The Three Rs

Have you ever heard of the three Rs? Reinforced Responses Recur. We believe children who demonstrate acts of self-discipline, manners, and courage deserve a reward because these tools lead to extraordinary personal safety. It may be a treat, like the dessert mentioned above, or it could be a few dollars when they perform an especially courageous act. Whatever rewards you choose, remember that rewards encourage more of the behavior you want to see.

Double Offers

We encourage you to develop double offers for behavior you see as vital to your child's safety. Teach your child that if a stranger (or someone she knows who gives her the creeps) ever offers her candy, money, or toys, or asks her to come with him when you are not around, tell that person "No," get away immediately, and come tell you. Passionately promise your child:

- I will double whatever that person offered you as a lure.
  (Example: If you are offered $20 to look for a lost dog in the woods, I'll give you $40 for saying "No," getting away, and telling me immediately.)
- You will not be in trouble … for getting away from trouble. In fact, I will reward your courage for not taking chances in a creepy situation.

You may be wondering, What do I do if my child lies and makes up stories to get double rewards? Odds are if that happens, it will only happen once because we are sure that you are not going to tolerate your child lying to you about important matters involving crime. From the many people who have given us feedback, we have not heard of one experience where children have abused this concept. We believe the reason for such success is the trust and respect that develops between Courage Coach and child due to honest discussion (not lectures) on these life-and-death matters.

The Rewards of Praise

Rewards don't always have to be tangible things. The least expensive reward is praise. Keep praise-filled compliments honest and sincere, with no more than 10 percent exaggeration. Kids are smart, and if you're not genuine, they will eventually figure out that insincere or severely exaggerated praise is just a form of manipulation. A limit of 10 percent exaggeration makes the dialogue fun and allows your child to know that the next level is possible, to accomplish a tougher feat or prevent a future risk. For example, "Wow, you really showed courage picking up our dog when that stray dog came into our yard. Your quick action prevented a dogfight and an expensive trip to the vet." In reality, you know the stray dog was probably just smelling the bushes in your yard several feet away. A 10 percent exaggeration in the compliment allows your child to visualize future consequences that were stopped because of the quick response.

Lending Library

Another nonmonetary reward system you might want to use involves a lending toy library. Use your children's supply of toys as a reward system for acts of courage. Rather than letting them have free access to all their toys at all times, consider a rotation system or lending toy library. When acts of courage are demonstrated, reward your child by saying, "Wow, Ben! Your manners and eye contact with that shoe salesman were terrific. When we get home you get to visit the toy closet!" Rotating a recently used toy (that needs to be boxed up properly) not only rewards your young child's courage, it keeps him excited by his abundant toy collection and teaches organizational tools. These benefits teach discipline and internal control skills, which are critical for safety decision-making. Your child will learn that delays are not denials. He learns to earn things rather than just get things. The courage to do the right things in life will often be without instant gratification.

Time Out in the Courage Corner

We saved our favorite courage-building tool for last! This tactic is so powerful, we bet it will become your favorite, too. Although this can be taught at about age 3, you will find that it is useful throughout your children's childhood up to and including their college years.

While disciplining our own kids, we recognized an opportunity to add a "courage twist" to the concept of Time Out (the practice of sending a child to a designated place for a certain amount of time as punishment for bad behavior). When your child misbehaves:

1. Send child to the Time-Out corner (or chair)

    The amount of time your child spends there is not important. The courage they need to earn permission to get out of the corner is what's important. Instead of watching the clock, monitor your child's breathing, giving him enough time to adjust his temperament.
2. Ask: "Are you ready to apologize so you can come out?"

    If child says, "No," let him stay longer until he says he is ready.

    If child says, "Yes," then go to him. Kneel down. Make sure your eyes are on the same level as his. Move close into his space. Grip his hands in yours. Stare him straight in the eyes.
3. Say, "Look me in the eyes. Now, what do you need to apologize for?"

    Odds are, the first time you do this your child will look down and start crying, overwhelmed at this level of communication intimacy. Great! Now it's time to teach courage!
4. Say, "Take a deep breath to control your tears. Keep gripping my hands and look me in the eyes. The only way I know you are telling me the truth is if you look through my eyes into my heart when you apologize without tears." Odds are, your young child will continue to struggle for self-control, incapable of speaking without tears.

5. Say, "It's OK! I can come back if you need more time" or "You can keep taking deep breaths and squeezing my hand until you are ready to see my heart through my eyes. Without tears, you need to apologize for _____." If your child continues to struggle, it is important for you to remain disciplined. Be gentle yet firm and use neutral facial expressions. Laughing or smiling will let your child off the hook. (You can laugh about this later—together!)

6. Repeat: "C'mon, you can do it! Take a deep breath and so on."

7. Welcome your child out of the corner when he can look you in the eyes throughout the entire apology, and apologize without crying. If crying starts, stop and give more time. Crying can be controlled by proper breathing and gripping (of a toy or their hands in a fist—open and close, open and close). You'll also want your child to provide a full-sentence apology for behavior that caused the Time Out. Example: "I'm sorry that I hit my sister." "I'm sorry that I hid my toys under the bed instead of putting them away in the box."

Time Out at Our Home

Our son Jimmy struggled terribly with Time-Out apologies when he was sent to the Courage Corner for bad behavior. This parental tool allowed us to identify an area in which our son hadn't mastered self-control. For Jimmy, the time part of Time Out didn't matter. The apology part was easy. It was the eye contact element that consistently weakened him to tears. It took us 2 full years, through preschool and kindergarten, to help him practice the verbal and emotional self-control he needed to earn his way out of Time Out and develop the life skill of self-control for recovery in a crisis. Obviously he hated Time Outs and adjusted his behavior as much as possible to make sure he was rarely sent there. Along the way, his mishaps allowed us priceless opportunities to develop much-needed life skills in him.

A Variation: Sibling Chivalry in the Courage Corner

When your children fight with each other (or with their good friends), send both (or more) to different Courage Corners for Time Out. The criteria needed to earn their way out of Time Outs are the same, with one small addition. They must both agree when they are ready to look into each other's hearts, by holding steady eye contact as they apologize to each other without tears (or laughter). Then, they need to repeat the same apology with consistent eye contact and no tears to you. A group hug is a wonderful reward.

Emergency Skills

Along with building a courage foundation, you can begin to teach and practice specific and critical safety skills with your 3-year-old. Help your child memorize:

- His own full name, address, and phone number with area code
- At least one grandparent's phone number with area code.
- At least one out-of-town relative or friend's name and phone number with area code (for the rare times local phone lines are damaged due to ice storms, tornados, hurricanes, forest fires, and so on).

Help your children memorize these phone numbers by allowing them to dial for you on your house line and especially your cell phone. Cell phones are lifesavers! In today's world, it is critical that young children know how to answer and dial out on cell phones too. Rest assured, this is not information overload. Your children will love that you trust them with the responsibility of being their "Dial Guy or Gal." They don't realize this is specific safety practice.

You need to also make sure your young children know your full legal name and their grandparent's full legal names. Kids often know key adults in their life as "Mom, Dad, Grandma, and Grandpa" yet do not know their legal names, especially if there are nicknames. Example: Grandpa's name is not really Jack, it's John Gardner.

At this stage, introduce children to the benefits of 9-1-1. Unplug a telephone and have your children practice dialing 9-1-1. Do this after a passionate explanation of the rare times it is appropriate to call the police, fire department, or an ambulance.

Pushing the buttons 9-1-1 is easy when children and adults are calm. Emergency dialing is extremely difficult when children and adults are upset or scared because oxygen and blood are rushing away from the hands, feet, and head. As your child's Courage Coach, create an occasional practice experience that is fun and that can test your children's self-control in a crisis. Have your children chase the dog, run around the house or the yard (anything that causes their breathing to increase and heart to pound), then give them a disconnected phone and say, "Quick, pretend there is an emergency. Pretend Mom fell down and broke her leg. Dial 9-1-1 and talk clearly to the operator." Kids love this kind of challenge. Be sure to debrief their response and reward their courage! End by saying, "You did a super job. If there is ever a real emergency, I know you will have the self-control to make brave decisions! I feel safe being around you." Put these words of confidence in your children's head and heart. Remember: Your children believe what you tell them!

7

SIZING UP SITUATIONS AND STAYING STRONG STARTING AT AGE 7

As your children mature, leave the age of innocence, and begin to understand life's dangers (around ages 7 or 8), you can begin to teach them the entire BST Family Defense message, adding the *T* as described in Chapter 5. The consequence of teaching *T*, for strike the throat, is serious, and needs to be taught when you feel your children are mature enough to understand its legal parameters as a last, desperate choice for real crime survival, *not* a playful tactic practiced on friends.

Keeping It in Perspective

We define mature adolescents as children around age 7 or 8 who can watch an occasional newscast without overreaction and nightmares. We are not suggesting that your children become news gurus at this age. We are suggesting that observation of your children's ability to keep scary news reports in perspective is a good test of anxiety level and emotional maturity. The occasional viewing of newscasts offers clever Courage Coaches an opportunity to observe what triggers their children's fear, as well as an opportunity to offer meaningful BST advice, especially when news stories relate to crimes against children (including violence of children harmed in their own homes).

Mature adolescents have the right and the need to know how to physically defend themselves as their personal freedoms expand (such as bike riding, sleepovers). Because their blossoming new behaviors will put them out of your sight, your children's expanded personal freedoms require expanded personal safety choices. This is why we encourage you, as your child reaches age 7 or 8, to start him or her practicing *T*—hitting the throat with rolled-up cardboard or paper towel tubes (as described in Chapter 5).

Continue Self-Control Lessons

Along with introducing the physical defense aspect of the BST Family Defense during this stage of your child's development, you need to also continue to emphasize the importance of self-control. By the age of 7 or 8, your children need to know and regularly practice the words that create the *B* summary of self-control, useful in any dangerous situation, especially crime scenarios:

> *Breathe* from the belly
> *Grip* your hands
> *Think Positively* (think of loved ones in violence)

In addition to the courage-building exercises we've presented in earlier chapters, there are a number of exercises relevant to kids in this age group—exercises that will build courageous and safe attitudes.

Make Watching Sports a Game

Watching professional sports on TV is an effective way to discuss safety-related self-control with your children. When TV cameras zoom in for close shots of key plays, encourage your children to watch athletes carefully as they attempt to perform their best under pressure.

Watch baseball with your kids. Baseball players don't just get off the bench, pick up a bat, and hit a baseball; they get off the bench and emotionally prepare to hit a baseball. Explain to your kids that because the players are nervous and/or scared (yes, failing has consequences), they go to the on-deck-circle where they warm up (move oxygen and blood to the right places). Have your children watch carefully as batters breathe deeply as they swing and grip the baseball bat. The batters then walk to the batter's box, breathing even deeper, with additional gripping adjustments of their cap, pants, and gloves. Look carefully with your children to see the players' concentration as they visualize (positive thoughts) where they want to hit the ball. Between each pitch, the entire routine—breathe, grip, visualize hit—is repeated.

Basketball players have a different routine rooted in the same self-control tools. These tools are especially visible when the players are shooting a foul shot. They take huge belly-breaths while bouncing the ball excessively (open-handed grip circulates blood), and they visualize the ball going in the basket before they shoot it. Some even pantomime the full shooting motion before they actually shoot the ball.

Expand your search beyond the world of sports. Actors and singers stand ready to perform behind the curtains, breathing and gripping to pump up the high energy necessary to reach the audience, especially the people in the back row. Actors and singers mentally rehearse their performance and visualize the applause from the audience (positive thoughts).

Besides professional performers, watch nonprofessionals too, especially during high-energy events like high school and college championship games and the Olympics. Children's theater and music performances also offer excellent opportunities to see peak performances and (nonviolent) tests of courage in action. A child's willingness to try a public performance is worthy of a standing ovation.

Positive Self-Talk

Postevent interviews and analyses are priceless opportunities for your children to learn the power of self-talk. Often, reporters ask athletes and performers questions such as "What were you thinking about?" or "What did your teammates say to each other?" in an attempt to understand peak performance under pressure. Make it a game for your children to find and tell you about instances of athletes and performers disclosing the importance of positive self-talk, what they said to themselves or others, as they were tested in emotionally charged (fear-filled) games.

When an athlete or performer falters, also have your children watch for disclosures of an athlete's negative self-talk and/or media commentators' statements such as "she appears to have lost her confidence" or "he's in a slump."

When you adjust your children's influence and awe of a professional athlete or performer from what they do to how they do it, not only will your children be inspired but they'll also realize that your guidance tools for self-control in any crisis are right on target!

Performance Scripts

Help your children adopt or create their own positive self-talk to survive times when they are afraid or uncomfortable. When you encourage your children to participate in academic, musical, theatrical, and athletic performances, you give your children back-door safety practice because self-confidence and courage are tested in all kinds of performances. When your child exhibits self-control, celebrate it and encourage her to identify her positive-self-talk:

Sarah, your concentration in that soccer game was just remarkable. Nothing got past you. And that's how you are in life! You sense trouble and confront it immediately. Even though your opponents were huge, they didn't intimidate you. Your will power, quick thinking, and courage inspire me. By the way, what did you say to yourself those last few minutes when the score was tied?

As your children's Courage Coach, you need to figure out how they think when they are afraid so you can wire them for high-quality performance self-talk!

The development of quality self-talk requires 3 P's. Words need to be:

Positive
Passionate (said with emotion)
Present tense

Positive Self-Talk Examples:

I'm OK ... Yeah! I'm OK. Right now.
Right now I can ... Yes! Yes! Hang on! Yes!
I (think) I can ... I can! I can! I can!
I'm doin' it! Yeah! I'm OK, I'm doin' it!

This is fun. Yeah! Go, go, go, go!
A little more, yeah! More, yeah! More, yeah!
Hang on. Get through this. Hang on. Hang on.

Negative Self-Talk Examples

I'll try (not present tense).
I'm going to be better (not present tense).
I will (not present tense).
This is a bad day.
I'm stupid.
I hate this.
This is embarrassing.
I don't want to be here.
I'm in big trouble now.
It doesn't matter anymore.
Whatever, nobody cares.
I shouldn't be here.
I can't do this.

Regardless of age, all athletes and performers win or lose based on the words they choose. We believe this concept is critical when children are coached in crime prevention and crime survival! Instilling your children with positive self-talk is a priceless, lifesaving tool. Imagine your child challenged by a criminal. Do you think her odds of saving her own life are improved with embedded self-talk from the positive or negative list of self-talk expressions? Starting today, practice positive self-talk phrases with your children, so they have at least one, repetitive and positive self-talk phrase to guide them through difficult times, especially violence.

Improve Test Taking

Do you children dread taking tests? Are they poor test takers, especially state-mandated tests? Guess what? Your children have performance anxiety—they are afraid of the test now, and poor performance scores, failure, and embarrassment later. Use test taking as a way to conquer fear. To help your children overcome their fear, teach them to do what athletes do for peak performance.

1. Belly-breathe before you start and several times during the test.
2. Grip a marker, glue stick, or fat pen in your nonwriting hand and grip it continuously through the test. (You may need to get permission for this in advance from the teacher. It is worth the explanation!)
3. Think of that paperwork as a puzzle (positive word), not a test.

The Power of Hope

Sometimes, in our seminars, people ask us if positive self-talk for self-defense is dangerous for children because it causes them to develop false confidence. We believe the term *false confidence* implies perceived future failure, and we encourage parents to examine that concern so that they don't unwittingly project these fears onto their children. Of course it's false confidence for a 10-year-old to believe he can perform laser surgery on grandma's eyes without going to medical school. But we do not believe it is false confidence for a 10-year-old to believe he can outsmart an abductor in a parking lot if he is empowered with our simple, learnable BST Family Defense skills. When parents teach their children age-appropriate self-control, crime prevention, and crime survival techniques, and practice these techniques with their children in real-world, non-violent environments, both parents and children begin to sincerely believe that they can survive a threatening situation, and their hope is extremely powerful.

One of our favorite statements is "sophisticated people call positive self-talk hope!" We all have offered hope, prayer, blind belief, positive thoughts, and, yes, false confidence to desperate people in time of need: crippled auto accident survivors, cancer patients, high school students waiting to be accepted in their first-choice college, and so on. Many people make it because of this energy. In contrast we know negativity offered to a person in crisis is likely to weaken or destroy efforts toward healing or success.

As our own children's Courage Coaches, we choose to believe that when faced with a crisis, our daughter and son will always find a way out of it.

More importantly, we know they know we feel this way about them. Our goal is that you grow to sincerely believe in your children's courage and ability to always find a way out of a bad situation. Let the critics call it false confidence. We know better. Children live up to or down to their parent's expectations, starting when they are very young.

We Can Do It

The famous poster "Rosie the Riveter" hangs in our office. It depicts a woman during World War II, with rolled-up sleeves flexing her arm muscles. "We Can Do It" is in the conversation bubble over her head reflecting her positive (3-P) self-talk and verbal encouragement for other women to join her for heavy work in the factory as the men went off to war. It's possible that critics of that time called this new attitude for women false confidence. If so, history proved them wrong. Positive attitude blended with positive action is the best hope for positive results.

The Courage Room

What do you want your kids to know and believe? We strongly suggest that you type it out, frame it, and hang it in a place where it can be seen every day. In our home, the room that displays our beliefs is the first-floor bathroom! We call it the "Courage Room."

Our Courage Room's walls are filled with inspirational quotes, outrageously fun or unique family photos, and various certificates that celebrate our kids' unique accomplishments. From floor to ceiling, everything coordinates because everything is framed in gold (cheap frames spray-painted gold). There are also dozens of quick-read quote books in baskets and on shelves.

We know for a fact that all visitors, especially our children, read when they have a few reflective moments to themselves. Because of repetition and high visibility, our kids have accidentally memorized many of the framed quotes. For that reason, we rearrange them often, putting what's most important in key locations, then add new inspirations as we find them. Homemade contributions and quotes deemed worthy of a golden frame by our children are priceless because it allows us to see the thoughts they value.

We strongly encourage you to create a Courage Room in your main bathroom or any room where your children spend a lot of time. Besides your children, Courage Rooms will influence all guests, especially your children's friends, by letting them know your family's values.

Lying for Self-Protection

During this developmental stage, it's important to introduce the value of lying for self-protection. We call it "Get Out of Danger Lies." For their safety, make sure your children know they have your permission to lie as a crime prevention tactic in order to get away from an orange situation, or anyone they know or don't know who gives them the creeps. Moving their hula-hoop space back while lying ("I don't have the time," "I don't know the directions," and so on) allows your children to escape conversation setups, which is the most prevalent style of attack against children.

Lying is a tough subject to discuss with clarity. On one hand, we do not want our kids to lie (except for safety), yet we all honestly know that everyone lies, to some degree, some of the time. Whenever topics are tricky to explain to kids, we recommend turning to our Behavior Flexibility Chart for clarity using the simple guidance of color.

Consider teaching the limits of lying using the colors gold, orange, and red (which also express the color of appropriate feelings connected with lying).

Gold Lies Make Others Feel Good

Share with your children that gold lies are OK to use on a limited basis because they help someone feel good.

- Sometimes it is more important to be kind than truthful.
  I love your new haircut, grandma!

- Sometimes the "truth hurts" and that pain is not necessary.
    Yes, I believe Santa is real!
- Sometimes truth ruins a surprise.
    OK, let's meet at my house [for a surprise birthday party] to go skating.

Golden lies are comments that children can feel good about.

Orange Lies Get You Out of Danger

Tell your child that orange lies are OK to use because they can help him avoid questionable circumstances and danger.

- Use to stop uncomfortable, unwanted conversations.
    I don't know those directions. I don't have the time.
    I don't want to try a cigarette. Smoke gives me asthma attacks (…even though I don't have asthma).
- Use to stop dangerous conversations.
    I didn't see your lost dog. I'm not allowed to leave the park and help you look for him.

Orange lies can make children feel powerful, clever, and safe.

Red Lies Cover Up Your Mistakes

Share with your children that red lies are wrong because people use them to cover up bad choices and behavior. Red lies are

- Used to cover up personal carelessness or laziness
    I swear I didn't cheat on the test.
    I didn't know the report was due today.
- Used to cover up dangerous bad choices
    I did not take money out of your wallet.
    I did not knock him down the steps.
    I did not try drugs at the party.

Red lies make your child feel bad about himself.

The Right Dose of Each Color

Too many golden lies can weaken family bonds and safety as loved ones find it difficult to predict and trust each other's honest thoughts and behavior. This is especially a problem when a family faces a crisis. "Well, I'm not sure that's what happened. You know she sugarcoats the truth to protect us all the time."

For improved safety and peace in your home, teach your children to be clever, to avoid conversations that set them up to tell gold lies whenever possible:

- When the discussion of grandma's new hairdo begins, walk out of the room. Just smile at grandma.
- When a little child asks about Santa, pretend you didn't hear the question and quickly change the subject.

Feel good instilling these powerful color-coded guidelines about lying. Gold lies are OK in small doses; orange lies are OK because they could save your life; and red lies are *never* acceptable in our family. For high character and safety, Courage Coaches need to make it clear that trust in your home is of paramount value.

Think-Feel-Do!

What you say and how you say it will have tremendous impact on your child's belief in herself. Children are often more influenced by emotion than by reason. Your child's self-esteem is her emotional opinion of herself.

You need to find the words and speak the language that will help your children's emotional opinion of themselves be as positively strong as possible. Courage Coaches are peak performance psychologists, too.

Because your children's words, thoughts, and feelings interact with each other, what they think, feel, and do creates their behavior. Positive thoughts, positive feelings, and positive words lead to positive action. While it is difficult to control your child's thoughts and feelings, you can help them control their words to influence their actions.

Speak Your Child's Language

Children (and adults) predominantly speak in one of three representational systems when they process their thoughts and formulate their sentences.[1] Those representational systems are as follows:

- *Visual:* They mostly use "seeing" words.
- *Auditory:* They mostly use "hearing" words.
- *Kinesthetic:* They mostly use "feeling" words.

When members of a family predominantly use different representation systems, miscommunication is common, especially when one is emotional or upset. Although the example below starts as a mild disagreement, miscommunication quickly becomes hurtful and can lead to danger when kids become teenagers and think, "I can't communicate with my parents. They don't understand me."

Visual-MOM: Tim, you look like a bum in that old shirt with the torn-off sleeves.

Kinesthetic-TIM: But Mom, it feels comfortable! (He silently continues with his feeling-driven self-talk "because it's the one my best friend gave me before he moved away.")

V-MOM: [getting upset] Don't you know your appearance is a reflection of our family?

K-TIM: [getting upset] I don't care about that (besides comfort, I care about the good memories/feelings I have when I wear it).

V-MOM: [losing control] How dare you not care about our family's image!

K-TIM: [leaves, slamming door to express feelings] (Self-talk: Why does she make me feel like this? I hate feeling like this.)

The example above is real-world miscommunication, typical of conversations in many homes. A careful diagnosis of key words used in the mother and son's miscommunication gives a good overall view of how two different ways of thinking conflict. Look carefully:

---

[1] Originally developed by Richard Bandler and John Grinder in Neuro-Linguistic Programming

The mom (V) predominantly values what she sees (V) and doesn't stop to think (V) about why her son (K) is emotionally (K) attached to an old comfy (K) shirt. The son (K) predominantly values what he feels (K) and doesn't understand why she cares about his appearance (V) instead of his feelings (K).

Neither the mom nor the son is right or wrong. They are different. Imagine the consequences of months and years of communicating like this. Does it become a safety factor? You bet it does.

You may be wondering, in the example above, what changes are needed to avoid such serious miscommunication. The change needed is a disciplined willingness to listen for key *words* that let you know which system your child values, then use that system to facilitate conversation. It's really not hard. In fact, it is fun.

We have created a short list, by category, of basic words for each way of thinking, so you can test the effectiveness of this deliberate way of communicating with your children, especially when they are upset. The first set of words in each category—see, hear, and feel—are the ones we encourage you to listen for and repeat back for peak communication with young children.

VISUAL	AUDITORY	KINESTHETIC
See	**Hear**	**Feel**
Picture	Sound	Hold
Look	Listen	Feel
Notice	Mention	Grasp
Observe	Discuss	Touch
Watch	Say	Hunch
Mind's eye	Loud and clear	In touch
See to it	Voice an opinion	Come to grips with it

Time Outs are a great place to practice using the right words to communicate accurately with your children. In our home we discovered we needed to use kinesthetic words to communicate with our son, such as, "What do you *feel* is the problem?" If we asked our son, "Do you see what you did wrong?" he would have no clue how to answer, especially when he was upset. He couldn't translate our visual words to explain his feelings.

When your children are upset, help them select the right words so they can communicate rapidly to recover. This is a tremendous self-control discipline for childhood that can be taken into their adult life.

CASH FOR COURAGE

As you know from previous advice, we believe in the concept of rewarding the behavior that you want. Starting at age 7, your children become consumers. They want things. Instead of buying them for your children, encourage your children to save for and buy things they want themselves. Allow your children to earn the extras through completion of chores (where they learn to help) and cash for courage.

The amount of money you offer as a reward per act does not matter. What matters is your consistent acknowledgment of their acts of kindness, courage, and bravery. Examples could be:

$10   Rapidly walking away from the creepy man who stopped his car in the neighborhood, wanting to lure you over for directions.

$10   Stopping your little sister from running in front of a car.

$ 5   Making quality eye contact, talking clearly and politely, and firmly shaking hands with dad's office coworkers.

$ 1   Finding inspiring self-talk in the sports page from an athlete who won a championship game.

$ 1   Picking up trash on the sidewalk rather than stepping over it (without being told).

$ 3   Finding a frame-worthy quote for the Courage Room.

Cash for courage is a wonderful teaching tool that will create great memories as well as give your children a chance to test their courage in real-life scenarios.

Real-Life Cash for Courage

At age 11, our daughter was confronted at a resort pool party by a teenager offering drugs. She was uncomfortable and immediately left with two friends. When her 8:00 P.M. curfew approached, she was heading alone toward our hotel room when the teenager jumped out and said, "What's the matter, did I scare you away before?" She said she stepped back (moved her hula-hoop space), pointed her finger at him, and said, "No, I am not afraid of you! Get away." With that he turned his head to see if anyone was looking, and she took off running and made it rapidly to our room. She wildly banged on the door. As we opened the door, she said, "I've finally seen red eyes; I know what you guys are talking about!" Our response, naturally, was "What happened?" She told us the story. Of course we were thrilled with her courage; it was her first real test. We paid her $50, which was all of our emergency hideaway cash. We gave it to her in honor of our Cash for Courage Agreement. She was shocked! She never saw a $50 bill before. About an hour later, she was brushing her teeth and stopped to ask us a question, "Am I allowed to sit by the pool tomorrow with my friends?" What a question. Whereas many parents would have said, "No," fearful that the teenager would be back, we said, "Yes" because we are Courage Coaches. Our daughter didn't do anything wrong. She did everything right and earned cash! In saying, "Yes, of course," we added, "Make sure you keep looking around for this creep tomorrow, Ms. Detective. If you see him, quickly come get us. We'd like to meet him."

Lengthening Their Security Blanket

Reasonable freedoms are starting to become part of your child's daily life. The courage skills you've practiced with her in the security of your presence may now need to be applied without you around. By adopting a family defense plan, you are teaching your child that she is never alone. She can remain connected with you by drawing strength from your belief in her. Keeping herself safe is doing what is best for the whole team: her family.

In the next chapter we are going to offer more exciting ideas to keep your children confident, strong, and safe during the challenging teen years.

8

BE SMART, BE STRONG, AND SURVIVE STARTING AT AGE 14 AND UP

Your children need to take risks. Without risks there are no rewards, and your children's full potential will never be reached. Your teenagers face unknown and potentially serious risks—successfully—every day. Will the car that is coming in the opposite direction stop for the red light? Will his answers be correct when the teacher calls on him? Will she be safe working evening or night shifts? Will his chicken be fully cooked at the restaurant? Is he safe flying in an airplane? Because your children have had frequent successful experiences in these activities, a level of comfort has developed. You (and they) feel assured that if tested again, good decisions will be made again. Frequency equals experience.

On the other hand, your teenagers do not have frequent experiences with high-risk behaviors such as walking alone in dark parking garages, hitchhiking, taking drugs, drinking alcohol, responding to a carjacking, and so on. When you take away frequency, you take away experience. With little or no experience in threatening crime scenarios, all your children have to rely on is their high character rooted in self-control skills and years of BST mental rehearsal, discussions (not lectures), and physical practice. (Starting at age 7, how many cardboard tube throats will your children crush by the time they are teenagers?)

Teaching your teens how to handle high-risk behaviors is a huge job. It's a lot tougher out there than when you were a teen. Since you can't imagine every possible scenario that may confront your children, you need to coach your children to believe that they can handle anything thrown at them. The best way to do that is to let them handle what is thrown at them—on their own.

Overcoming Daily Challenges

Kids are used to hitting the "escape" or "new game" buttons on their computer games when things are not going in their favor. Life isn't that simple. As your children grow older, you'll need to step back and rescue them less—to help prepare them to protect themselves. Yes, we know it can be hard. But remember, we didn't learn to walk without falling down. If we were never allowed to fall, we wouldn't learn balance.

Allow your teenagers to progressively solve their own problems. You want your children to have frequent experiences at overcoming daily adversities so they can draw upon these strategies for future, more threatening challenges. Think, for a moment, about the process of learning to drive. When we experience fog, slippery roads, wet leaves, and so on, we accumulate experiences that build our confidence to handle future driving challenges like thunderstorms and black ice. The same goes for development of problem-solving and self-protection skills.

When our brains perceive difficult situations as being manageable, chemicals such as cortisol and noradrenaline energize us and keep us from suffering the psychology of defeat. When your children have to depend on themselves to overcome challenges, they draw upon their accumulated past experiences and skills just like the rest of us do. They then develop adaptive expertise—the ability to emotionally and physically respond quickly and appropriately in later situations.

Even though we don't want our children to have even one experience that deals with critical emergencies such as violence, we can't protect them all the time. It's vital that they have a database of decision-making successes and failures derived from less-than-threatening scenarios, so that they have the skills to survive (potentially) lethal scenarios.

Practicing BST Responses

While laying the foundation for smart decision-making, continue to give your teenagers mental rehearsal practice in response to pertinent news-related critical incidents. Now that your children are teens, they are watching more intense (yes, violent) dramas on TV, DVDs, or videos that raise serious issues worthy of insightful discussions. Ask your child if he knows a better response. If possible, pause the DVD or tape and role-play with him. Keep it fun and lively. If the fight scenes are ridiculous, make fun of them!

Ask your teen, "So, Ashley, what would you do in that situation? You're a brave person ..."

- Include the brave label because it lets her know that you know that she already knows what to do.
- If you do not include the complimentary label, you are likely to get no response, or a low-energy response from a teen.

After she answers with BST foundation choices, say, "Awesome! You can do it. You'll find a way!" That response is a "Courage Command"— a coaching phrase from you that your child will have planted in her mind after years of repetition. In a crisis, she'll replay that command and be reminded of her ability. Keep it brief. Say it passionately and sincerely. Make it memorable, like catchy refrains of songs.

Using the BST strategies you have learned so far, create muscle memory by having your kids playfully show you how they would respond. Include mental, verbal, and physical responses in your re-creations. The best substitute for experience to prepare your child for crisis survival is passionate, consistent, and fun Courage Coaching by you.

If you find during a rehearsal practice that your teen needs direction on what to do, give that guidance in the shortest discussion possible, emphasizing key points. Use *do* or *you can* comments when teaching.

- Avoid preaching.
- Avoid *do not* statements. The brain has a hard time processing a negative command or statement. Have you ever noticed when you shout out to a teen, "Do not spill your drink!" they almost

always do? That is because their brain has to first think about spilling the drink so it can then take the necessary action not to do it. Confused? ... Then do *not* think about a pickle. Ha! You just did it, and your mouth is watering from the stimulus of what we just said not to do. Here is the moral of the story: Ask for what you want, not for what you don't want. Example: "Be careful with your drink."

Your Teenager's Learning Process

As you let your teenagers make their own decisions and mistakes, avoid being judgmental. Praise their courageous efforts in trying, rather than focusing only on the outcome. As they grow older they will discover how their choices affect outcomes. Allowing them to make measurable progress forward, while experiencing the sting of occasional setbacks, is key to their future independence and quality decision-making. In other words, stop rescuing your teenager from discomforts caused by their poor decision-making.

Be careful not to enable carelessness. At this age, no more forgotten homework rushed to school. No more defensive arguments with teachers if your child is corrected for bad behavior. No more disruption of your schedule to accommodate your child's plea from school, "I forgot to tell you to pick me up earlier today."

Patterns of carelessness can lead to personal weakness. Personal weakness is a serious safety issue. Personal weakness makes your child more of a target for criminals, unhealthy friends, dates, spouses, bosses, and so on. Turn your "I forgot..." (dependent) teenager, into an "I'll find a way" (independent) teenager.

Checking Up on Teens

When you consistently say to your teenager, "Call me when you get there" or "I worry about you," your teen translates your words to mean: "You don't trust me" or "You don't believe I can handle myself." Yes, you are worried about your child, and you say those things because you love her. However, these types of statements over a long period of time can diminish a teenager's sense of personal control and positive self-talk, as well as cause her to doubt her ability. (We commonly talk to women in their 40s and 50s who still have loving/controlling parents who want to be called to make sure they got home OK.) We believe requesting report-in calls—every day, every time, from everywhere is too much. Reward your teenager's responsibility, based on age, with less frequent call-in reporting for every move they make. Learn to assume they will make it home safely, because with your belief in them, odds are high they will!

The affordability of cell phones has helped this parenting dilemma tremendously in the past few years. It's likely that your kids have cell phones or have access to other people's cell phones. If you're a little anxious about your teenager's safety while she is traveling a longer than usual distance or if the weather is bad, call the number at her destination to pretend you forgot to tell her something. You don't need to do this on a regular basis, only when you have a heightened concern—infrequency will make this tactic less obvious.

As your teen is on the way out the door, instead of saying, "I worry about you," simply say, "I love you."

Setting Boundaries

It's OK to still set rules and refuse to allow certain behaviors with your teenager. What if he responds to this refusal to allow a certain behavior (for example, staying overnight at a boy/girl party) with "Don't you trust me?" Your response is, "Yes, I trust you! It's not your intentions or goodness that are in doubt. It's just your inexperience to control your behavior under the influence of feelings whose power you do not yet fully understand."

Sometimes you will be betrayed and let down. Your children won't be perfect. It would be boring if they were. Through your courage coaching and modeling, though, hopefully their mistakes will only be mistakes of the head and not mistakes of the heart.

The phrases *mistake of the head* and *mistake of the heart* were part of the police ethics class Mike taught for years. Mistakes of the head are brainy: overslept, forgot something, misspelled a word, daydreaming, and so on. Mistakes of the heart are rooted in not caring. Doing unethical, immoral, or illegal activities are mistakes of the heart. If your trust is broken by your teenager, determine if it was of the head or of the heart. If it was a mistake of the head, let your teen suffer the consequences (being late, missing school assignment, going without lunch). If it was a mistake of the heart, render an appropriate punishment for the specific act and get back to trusting again.

Mentors

In their search for themselves, your teens may express their core values in ways that you don't agree with—hairstyle, clothing, political views, music, friends, and so on. Occasionally you and your teen may have a battle of wills, and you will need help. It's natural for teenagers to rebel a little, so when someone else they trust advises them, they'll likely listen. Find a backup adult in your child's life who will stop and listen to them—a mentor.

A mentor is like an assistant Courage Coach taking care of your child but just not as directly. Aunts, uncles, or family friends can be mentors. Whoever you ask to watch out for your teen, look for someone who can:

- Listen without interruption or judgment
- Remind your child of positive gifts and strengths
- Encourage forgiveness of self for mistakes
- Encourage forgiveness of others for their shortcomings and imperfections
- Offer advice, if asked for it, in as few words as possible

Have your teen's mentor intervene through chance meetings. We called our son's baseball coach once and asked him to bump into Jimmy in the hallway to see how Jimmy was doing after a confrontation with his basketball coach. This baseball coach was honored and helped Jimmy deal with the issue.

Depending on the relationships your children have with these other adults in their lives, you can ask them to directly intervene, if necessary.

We use the mistake of the head or mistake of the heart as the gauge for whether or not we expect a mentor to report back to us. We are still our children's primary teachers. Any behavior that would put your child in danger needs to be reported back to you by the mentor.

Overcome the Psychology of Defeat

Help your teenager learn to live without compromising himself. If your teen participates in sports, lifts weights, jogs, or does other exercise, make sure that you teach him to overcome complacency by encouraging him to periodically work out, even when he doesn't feel like it. Teach your teenagers that their brains and bodies should not surrender every time they're too tired, frustrated, or irritable to work out. Frequent experience at overcoming adversity and physically making demands of themselves when fatigued will give them references to draw upon in future adversities. The familiar slogan—when the going gets tough, the tough get going—needs to be practiced. To help your teen, join in on taking a run around the neighborhood or working out in the gym.

Peer Pressure

Our children sometimes choose friends who have a little wild side. We believe it's their substitute for being a little wild themselves. Though they may not admit it, your teen's friends probably chose him to hang around with because they want someone who will make good decisions and not follow the crowd. However, your teenager can influence other teens as much or more than other teens can influence your child. Your child can be the one to lead friends with courageous decision-making.

Teach your teenager that negative peer pressure comes from people who don't really feel good about themselves and what they are doing, so they try to get others to go along with them. Let your teen know that agreeing to do something he does not really want to do or feel good about doing does not change his friends' feelings about themselves.

Encourage your child to respond to negative peer pressure with short, firm command-type statements and then to walk away. To give your teen practice, use acting games like charades. You can make the entire game up replacing usual scenarios with situations relevant to your child's current experiences or just insert one every once in a while. Under the umbrella of family fun, have your child act out the following scripts. Check for belly-breathing, gripping, strong eye contact, and confident tone of voice.

"How about a cigarette?"   "No, Thank You!"
"Let's go sneak some beer."   "I don't want to."
"You wanna smoke some weed?"   "Forget it."
"C'mon chicken, try some Ecstasy."   "Back off!"

Ask your child to come up with some of her own peer pressure statements. The key is for your child to courageously respond with short, firm statements.

You also may want to consider providing your teen with an out if his friend or the group tries to override his decision not to participate in a high-risk activity. Let your teen know he can have you be the bad guy. Have your child say, "I am not going to do XYZ. If my parents/dad/mom find out, it will not be worth it. I'll be busted. You guys don't want that to happen, do you?" Let your child know he can save a little face by using you as the scapegoat.

Drinking, Drugs, and Dating—New Challenges for Your Teen

As your children start going to dances and parties, they will be exposed more and more to alcohol and drugs. The purpose of this book is not to encourage you to lecture your children about the dangers of chemical abuse. We want to give you ways to empower your child to resist the pressure to participate. Your children will be presented with a series of complex challenges as they grow older, and the courage foundation you've worked to build in them will help them make decisions that keep them safe.

Discuss drug abuse with your teenagers. Rather than lecture them about drugs, impress upon them the lack of control and the weakness they will experience when they either knowingly or unknowingly use drugs. Turn your child into the teacher. Reverse roles and have your teen pressure you with comments so that you can respond with firm, short commands, modeling the behavior you'd like to see in them.

Educate your children about date rape drugs such as Rohypnol. The pill is dropped into the victim's drink or food when she's not looking or leaves the table. Rohypnol looks like aspirin—small, white, and round. GHB is another date rape drug. GHB is a clear liquid but could also be a white powder. Encourage your teens to always be careful with their food and drink at parties. Teach them to maintain control over these items and if they cannot, throw them away and get fresh ones. Tell them not to accept any drink or food they haven't prepared themselves.

Our daughter offered us this wonderful idea while in high school. She and many friends actually took their own cups with twist lids to parties (like those used to hold coffee in the car) to reduce the likelihood of someone quickly dropping foreign substances in their drinks.

When your teenage daughter begins to go on dates, rather than lecture the boy about his behavior, tell him that you expect him to make sure that your daughter does not ride with anyone who drinks or uses drugs. Transfer some responsibility to the boy with this command—he is included in his own assignment!

College-Bound Teens

Many parents get very concerned about the safety of their teenagers when they transition from high school to college, because many students live away from home, even out of town. However, your anxiety can be lessened if you're willing to give your teens more and more responsibilities as they grow up.

If you're reading this book to teach a teenage child going off to college, don't skip the earlier chapters. Just create an accelerated version of teaching them BST. Repetition is good for learning but passion is even better. You can greatly impact your college-bound teenager's courage by passionately teaching the BST strategies contained in this book. Wave your Love Hand every time they leave home for college as you empower them with specific words of encouragement like: *Be brave! You know I believe in you!*

In addition, make sure you tell your child that you are willing to lose everything that you own for the privilege of defending her and her righteous decisions in court if necessary. This statement puts a steel rod down your children's spine. Besides your belief in them, they will respect the awesome trust that you have placed in their decision-making. Even under extreme pressure, they will not make mistakes of the heart. You just want them to do whatever it takes to stay safe and come home!

When your college students report upcoming participation in an event that you feel might involve danger (like traveling with friends or sorority/fraternity members to a conference or visit in a large dangerous city), refrain from saying what your Mother might have said to you: *That's a dangerous place, I wish you wouldn't go!* Instead, recognize that college students are adults and are probably going to do what they want to do, with or without your permission. We recommend that you acknowledge the danger you fear with *color* and then remind them of their power: *I've been to (or read about) downtown _____(city) and it can be an orange place by day, and a red place by night. I know you can handle any challenge that might surface. I do ask that you to keep a close eye on your friends. I am not sure they have mastered their courage switch the way you have!* This is a clever way to alert your young adults to danger you know exists, compliment their courage, and put them in the position of heightened responsibility—watching over their friends (which naturally will intensify their awareness!)

The best advice we have to offer for raising courageous teens: Love your child enough to tell her what she needs to hear, whether or not she wants to hear it. Be brief. Color-code dangers. Passionately remind her of her rights, responsibility and courage. A BST Family Defense foundation will help your teen move through these difficult years courageously and confidently, allowing you to feel the same.

PART 4

THE FAMILY DEFENSE PLAN IN ACTION

9

THE FAMILY DEFENSE PLAN AT HOME

In this chapter, you'll find advice and strategies for courage scenarios in your home. You'll find ways to teach your child how to keep safe and in control. Even though we cannot possibly cover every scenario that may occur, with a BST foundation, your child can develop adaptive expertise and the life-saving belief that he can control, manage, and, at the least, survive any critical incident at home.

Discuss these scenarios with your children, role-play their application of BST principles, and teach them how to mentally rehearse their responses. For the strongest impact on your children's critical thinking skills, make sure their mental rehearsals are in motion, with sound— like a movie. Ask your child prompting questions to facilitate this kind of thinking: What are the sounds you hear? What does your heart feel like? What are you thinking? What are you doing with your hands? These types of rehearsals activate the thinking brain and are sensory-rich with sights, sounds, and feelings.

Responding to Challenges Home

Teach your child to use the green/yellow/red traffic light concept to make rapid decisions during a critical incident at home. The green/yellow/red light concept is a conceptual method of providing your child with key strategies for rapid decision-making—situations in which

Home Alone

Most states do not have laws that state at what exact age a child must be before he can be left home alone or under the care of another child. There are general laws that require adequate and appropriate supervision of children. Most family service agencies use the following criteria as guidelines for determining whether or not a child can be home alone:

- The maturity level of the child
- The accessibility of the parent, guardian, caretaker, or responsible adult by phone or in person
- The physical or mental health condition of the children
- The behavioral history of the children
- Whether a young child is using a stove, iron, or appliance that poses a danger because of his age
- Whether the residence has smoke detectors
- Whether there are unusual hazards in the home
- The children's reaction to being left alone
- The ages of the children being cared for
- Whether the child has completed a babysitting course
- The reliability of the person that the parent has chosen to provide supervision

Some states will consider the following age ranges and time left alone as criteria for investigating child endangerment:

- Children 7 and under left alone for any period of time
- Children ages 8 and 9 who are alone for more than 2 hours
- Children 10 through 13 who are left alone for more than 12 hours
- Children 14 to 17 who are unsupervised while parents are absent for more than 24 hours

You can use these guidelines when deciding whether or not your child is old enough to stay home alone or to babysit siblings or neighbors.

there is no discretionary time for him to ask someone else for help. Remember Hick's Law: The more choices in a crisis, the slower the reaction time.

The three-color traffic light system categorizes every possible situation as:

Green: Go—get out
Red: Stop—stay put
Yellow: Caution—proceed with caution

Most situations will require either a green (get out) or red (stay put) response. In situations in which your children can ask for help from you or another trusted authority over the phone, they're proceeding with caution (yellow) until you advise them to either go or stay.

Green Situations: Go!

If the situation is green, your child needs to get out of the house as quickly as possible. Green scenarios include smelling smoke, natural gas, or unusual fumes, or thinking there is a fire or someone breaking into the house. Designate a neighbor or a safe place for your child to go in a green situation. Depending on your neighborhood and whether or not other homes are close by, it may be a neighbor's house or a neighborhood grocer you know and trust. In green situations, encourage your child to run to safety and call 9-1-1. Your child's response to a fire, gas leak, chemical spill, or intruder is to GO green.

Sometimes, your child may not be able to easily flee through a ground-floor door. Depending on your home's layout, rehearse escape from the second story or the basement. Consider portable rope ladders for second-story rooms or teach your child to create rope ladders out of sheets or extension cords, if desperate.

There are times when it might be necessary for your child to jump from a second-story window if other routes aren't possible. Through your courage coaching, inspire your child to overcome any fear of needing to jump. While it may seem scary to encourage your children to jump, most falls from a second story are survivable and the odds of surviving are better than staying in a burning house. Some people have died in fires because they were too afraid to jump from even slight heights. Since the thought of jumping out a second-story window may be overwhelming in a calm setting, have your children mentally rehearse by imagining themselves jumping out of the window if the situation is desperate. With this kind of practice, in the unlikely event of a fire, the actions necessary for your child to increase survival chances are already implanted in his brain.

Home Break-In/Burglary

Most home burglaries are committed by thieves during daytime hours when they believe no one is home. If your child is home alone due to illness, school closing, and so on, teach her to make it obvious that someone is home by playing a television or radio. In the unlikely event that a burglar does break into your home, his intent is theft. If your child cannot get out of the house, teach her to lock herself in a room with a phone. Tell her not to resist the burglar if the burglar is only interested in stealing.

Consider teaching the following verbal tactic to your child if she is spotted by the burglar: "The alarm just went off; take what you want and hurry up and get out of here" or "My parents will be here any minute; hurry up and get out of here."

Red Situations: Stop!

The following situations warrant a red–stop response: severe storm, tornado, or a news report of a wild animal loose in the area or a crime that's just occurred. On hearing about such a situation, your child needs to make sure all doors and windows are locked. Red–stay put responses are for when the danger is *outside* the home. Your child uses the home to fortify his space from an outside threat.

Rehearse with your child a predetermined safe location inside your home for him to go to in case of a red situation (for example, the basement during a storm). If possible, have him take a cell phone with him or at least a portable phone. Teach him to stay off the phone during severe weather but to have it available for further instructions once the storm passes. In case of a news report or a phone call from a neighbor or you regarding a wild animal or criminal loose in the area, have your child keep in phone contact with you or another trusted person for instructions. Charged cell phones are preferred and may be the only phones that work if power lines are down in the area. Make sure your child knows the long-distance phone number of an out-of-town relative or friend in case of a widespread power outage. In any of these situations, you or other trusted adults in your child's life need to return home as soon as safely possible to be with your child.

Yellow Situations: Caution ...

Yellow lights—proceed with caution—are for situations where the threat is unknown. Something unusual is occurring but your child isn't exactly sure yet what to do.

Yellow light cautions can include minor injuries (cuts, scrapes, bruises, minor burns, and so on) or noises from the furnace. Your child can handle minor emergencies by belly-breathing, stopping minor bleeding with bandages, or icing bumps, bruises, or burns if needed, and calling you (or other responsible adult) for assistance without panicking.

Some yellow-light cautions merit special advice, such as strangers at the door or unusual phone calls.

Someone at the Door

Teach your children not to open the door for anyone they do not know or know but don't feel comfortable allowing in the house. If someone comes to the door asking to come in to use the phone to call for help (for example, because he has a broken-down car or is lost) teach your child to yell through the locked door that she, your child, will call the police for the person outside. Tell your child to call the police and to not feel ashamed to emphasize to the police that she is frightened. Instruct your child to then call you or another responsible adult.

Incoming Phone Calls

Rehearse how you want your child to handle incoming phone calls. If you have caller ID, consider having your child screen calls before he even answers the phone. Any unknown caller can be ignored or allowed to go to the answering machine.

If your child does answer the phone, instruct him to *never* disclose that he is home alone. Have your child tell the caller that mom or dad can't come to the phone right now and he'll take a message. Also teach your child to not give out any information to an unknown caller (phone number, address, personal information, and so on). Instead, have your child tell the caller that mom and dad will call back. Keep the conversations short. Your child can be respectful but firm.

If your child receives a prank, obscene, or threatening phone call, teach your child to tap on the phone mouthpiece with a pencil or even their finger and say, "Officer, this is the call," and hang up immediately. Create the illusion that the police are tapping the phone. Tell your child to then call you or another responsible adult right away.

Being a Babysitter in Other People's Homes

When babysitting, your child can apply the same green/yellow/red responses to a critical incident as if she was home alone. Before allowing your child to babysit at someone else's home, we recommend that you meet the parents of the child at their home. So you will know that your child will have the necessary information and tools to protect herself and the client's child, ask the following questions:

- Will the parents be available immediately by phone?
- Are there any items in the home that may be hazardous (for example, chemicals, fuels, pets, guns)?
- Are there smoke detectors, escape methods from upper stories, or the basement area? Does the home have an alarm system (burglar and/or fire)?
- Will a trusted neighbor be home during the time my child is babysitting?
- Is their home in a 9-1-1 emergency call area?

Unless your child is absolutely sure of the home's address, recommend that the address be posted by the telephone so that your child can tell a dispatcher the address without hesitation. If you are comfortable with the other parents and their home, tell the other parents (in the presence of your child) of your confidence in your child's ability to manage an unlikely critical incident. Your belief in your child will not only give the clients added peace of mind, it will add to your child's belief in her critical thinking skills.

Being with a Babysitter in Your Home

Apply the above babysitter tactics in reverse when your child is being watched. If the babysitter is coming to your home, ask her parents to meet with you in your home and go through the above checklist with them. Introduce your child to the babysitter in this pre-visit. In front of the babysitter, her parents, and your child (depending on your child's maturity and B and S skill level), praise your child's self-control and space awareness abilities. If your child is being babysat at the sitter's home, go to her home, meet her family, and ask the questions covered in "Being a Babysitter in Other People's Homes."

Assess the potential babysitter's maturity level during your visit. Ask for references. Watch how your child interacts with the sitter. Abusive sitters are rare. Your main concern is that the sitter will neglect her duty—watch TV or do her own thing without paying proper attention to your child. Meeting with a potential sitter and her family and going through your checklist will convince you whether or not you can trust your child to her care.

Being with Friends and Relatives

In order to keep your children's feelings about safety consistent, you need to devise a game plan for handling friendly gestures of hugging, kissing, touching, wrestling, and dancing at family events. We don't want you to feel paranoid about your children interacting with family members at get-togethers. Relatives' sincere gestures of fun and affection do not have to be curtailed because of safety issues. However, teach your children that they have total control over what happens inside of their space. Except for health reasons (doctors and dentists), when you are there to condone intrusion of your child's space, no one, whether your child knows them or not, has the right to get inside your child's space without permission.

Before the family get-together, tell your children who might be there, and if you have any upfront concerns about anyone, share that with your child. Tell your child, "Uncle Ted might be there and he likes to wrestle around. He doesn't mean anything bad by it but if he gives you the creeps, tell him to stop. We will respect and support you."

Teach your children that they have your permission to tell anyone to keep out of their space by saying things like, "Please don't tickle me right now," "Please, I don't want to wrestle right now." Make sure that you stand behind your child's wishes by not confusing them with, "It's OK, it's just Uncle Ted...." If you see that your child's "No" is not being respected, jump in and end whatever game is being played. You don't have to be rude, but be firm. Say something like, "Uncle Ted, Johnny says to stop … it's over."

Gun Sightings

We encourage you to tell your young children that if they ever see someone (adult or child) show what appears to be a gun (green—go), to immediately come home and tell you. The reward is an immediate visit to the toy store where they can choose any toy in the store, including an expensive bike or dollhouse. This is the exact offering we made to our children. Thankfully, we never needed to make a payoff.

As a police family with many firearms in our home, we know the importance of keeping guns empty, locked up, and out of everyone's view, especially children. This is a nonnegotiable rule. We expect all adults (and their children) to have the same discipline and respect for firearms. We want nothing to do with families or children who do not live by this high safety standard. Nor should you.

Your children's eyes provide views into the everyday world of neighbors and friends that you may never see as an adult. If guns are out in the open, innocently or ignorantly, you do not want your child around that gun owner, his home, or his children. Period. Here is an example of what we said to our children:

You are a smart kid who knows right from wrong. If you ever see an adult or a child with a gun (or what appears to be a gun), run away and come tell me as much or as little as you want. I will not yell at you or ask you any questions. We will go straight to the toy store and buy you any toy that you want. Guns, real or fake, are big trouble and you'll get a big reward for getting away. Yes, the exception is water guns. I know you can tell the difference because water guns are brightly colored orange, green, or yellow plastic toys. If you are not sure, just get away.

Reviewing Responses

With the green/yellow/red response concept, your children will be reminded of the principles every time they see a traffic signal. When you are in your car with your child, take the opportunity every once in a while to review the green/yellow/red principles. At a red light, ask her what are some red–stop, stay put situations? Teach your child that if there is some time to make a decision, ask someone they trust what to do. If immediate action is necessary, either get out (green–go) or stay in (red–stop).

Trust in yourself that you are raising a child who knows how to keep a home safe, and how to stay safe at home.

10

THE FAMILY DEFENSE PLAN
AT SCHOOL

The good news is that gun control laws, smaller classes, anti-bullying programs, character programs, and Safe School Plans *are* having a concrete impact on violence in schools. However, we still have work to do—from the everyday reality of bullying to the worst-case scenario of students with guns. This chapter will provide you with specific ways you can teach your child to apply BST principles so that she can be in command of her own personal safety while going to or from, or being at, school.

Protecting Yourself From Bullies

Even though schools do what they can to encourage and enforce good behavior, there are still times when your child needs to take responsibility for his own safety. Many schools have and enforce Codes of Behavior to deal with inappropriate actions. Some schools have a full- or part-time school resource officer who works with school staff and students on a daily basis. However, there are times when your child must use his self-confidence and self-reliance to control a situation at school. The most common negative situations that your child might have to control are issues surrounding bullying.

Bullying is a term that has been used to describe a wide range of behaviors, from disrespect to teasing and harassment to criminal acts. No matter what label or level of bullying it is, if someone is *creating fear* in your child it is not just part of growing up nor can it be dismissed by saying, "kids will be kids." It's serious stuff. If your child is the victim of unprovoked aggression, it is a crime. Most schools have zero tolerance for fights and punish all parties involved if there is no clear evidence of who assaulted whom.

We're going to offer some additional applications of BST skills to enhance your child's strength and reduce the likelihood of being assaulted. These additional space protection and verbal skills are designed to avoid a physical altercation. If your child has tried every other avenue of stopping an altercation and isn't getting results, there are simple physical choices he can make that are less likely to harm the assailant but can still stop an altercation.

We believe that your courage coaching, a strong BST foundation, and practicing the school scenarios in this chapter will help to eliminate fears your child may have about being harmed at school.

Low-Fat Communication

If your child is a victim of bullying, ask him to describe his challenges using concrete, specific words. To get precise understanding of exactly what your child is telling you, use the following communication tactic, one we've used in police work to get to the bottom of an issue. Whenever your child uses general or "fat" nouns or verbs, ask him to be more specific. Ask your child: "*Who specifically...?*", "*How specifically...?*", "*What specifically...?*"

For example:

Child: "They're always picking on me."
Courage Coach: "Who specifically is always picking on you?"
Child: "Johnny Smith and Mary Jones."
Courage Coach: "How specifically are Johnny and Mary picking on you?"
Child: "Johnny and Mary are calling me names."
Courage Coach: "What specifically are Johnny and Mary saying?"
Child: "Johnny and Mary say I'm fat and ugly."

Now you know precisely what the challenge is for your child. Once you know exactly what the issue is for your child, you can determine your next course of action. If your child is a victim of crime, you can contact the police for next steps. If your child is being teased, harassed, or feels threatened, teach her the specific BST applications in this chapter.

Moving to Action with Verbal Techniques

Encourage your child to practice the "art of fighting without fighting." The best way to win a fight is to avoid one. By having a strong belief in their ability to handle a worst-case scenario, your children will be able to courageously apply nonverbal and verbal communication skills to deal with conflict. When you feel confident, you act confidently.

Start with a slightly adjusted three-word self-control plan:

1. Belly-breathe (move air)
2. Grip hands or object (move blood)
3. Show strong eye contact (positive determination!)

The first defense against a bully is your child's ability to control fear. If your child specifically describes bullying behavior as disrespect, teach your child to belly-breathe, grip, use strong eye contact and voice control, and say, "Stop disrespecting me!" If low levels of bullying such as teasing and harassment, and so on, can't cause fear in your child, then the bullying has no impact. Bullies only succeed if they can cause fear. Your child's self-control concepts (belly-breathing, gripping, and ability to hold eye contact) will go a long way to prevent his being bullied in the first place.

Just as your child needs belief in his ability to manage and handle critical situations, he also needs strong communication skills to protect herself. Simply being able to talk during a threatening event keeps the thinking brain activated and prevents fear from taking over.

There are several specific verbal tactics you can share with your child in hopes of stopping bullying and preventing a physical attack,

Ask/Tell/Demand Arm Motions during Confrontations

Body language and voice control account for over 90 percent of face-to-face communication. Use *gold, orange,* or *red* arm and hand motions to visually show escalation in a confrontation.

ASK

With strong eye contact and a calm, nonthreatening voice ask the disrespectful person to stop his behavior. Show your child how to ask by using the *golden* hand position—"preacher hands." His arms should be outstretched with his hands turned palms up. Preacher hands (so named because of the hand gestures used by religious leaders) symbolically display nonthreatening, open sincerity. Again, body language and voice control count for over 90 percent of face-to-face communication.

TELL

If the verbal assaults continue, teach your child how to escalate to an *orange* level by telling the person to stop. Have your child outstretch his arms with his palms down (as if he was touching the end of his personal hula-hoop space line with outstretched fingers). This arm/hand position claims your child's full personal space. In an attempt to stop the disrespectful person, say, "I'm telling you to leave me alone!"

DEMAND

If the disrespectful person continues and your child feels he is going to be physically attacked, tell him to *move back* immediately. While moving back teach your child to keep his arms outstretched as he adjusts his hands (the standing push-up position) to look like *red* "stop signs." With his hands up and in a loud, firm tone of voice, teach your child to say, "I *demand* that you stop." Your child can also try the following:

- *The Look, Lift, Lean Eye Contact Principle:* Look the disrespectful person straight in the eyes or at the eyebrows, lean slightly forward, lift your eyebrows, and say, "Is there anything that I can say or do to get you to stop?" (This body language adds to your child's display of confidence and sincerity.)
- *Word Salad:* Instead of attacking, moving back, pleading, or debating a verbal attack, teach your child to respond to the verbal attack with a string of phrases to bore the attacker. (An example might be "You know, I never really thought about that, but it may be from when I was in third grade and my teacher, Miss Smith, or was it Ms. Jones … was giving a class on …"). Using nonsense dialogue keeps your child breathing, shows he's not going to play the game

of reacting to the verbal attack, and lets the verbal attacker know your child is not willing to be a victim. This technique is done in a straightforward manner, with a wide hula-hoop of space, without sarcasm.

- *Using Humor to Diffuse Verbal Attacks:* Throwing back humorous comments at a verbal attacker can work as a diversionary tactic. Humorous comeback comments such as "yeah, I'm a nerd, I've been working on that" or "thanks, I'm trying to get into the Loser Hall of Fame" need to be said with strong eye contact and/or voice control, plenty of space—even while walking away—in a nonsarcastic tone of voice. Sarcasm is threatening. While stepping back to increase personal space, the use of appropriate humor, coupled with confident body language, voice tone, and large space can be disarming.

- *Dragnet Routine:* Just the facts. You and your children can get some laughs while teaching them how to keep personal feelings out of responses—a just-the-facts routine. Rent or buy DVDs or videos of the old *Dragnet* TV shows and watch how the police officers provide unemotional responses. Your children can use similar depersonalization techniques to keep verbal conflicts from boiling over into personal attacks. If someone says, "I don't like the way you ...", your child could respond with a nonpersonal statement such as "a lot of people don't like the way some people ...". Keep personal pronouns such as *I* and *you* out of the exchange.

The key to any verbal self-defense is having courage. If your child responds nervously or is uncertain of his ability to handle himself should the verbal attacker become physical, no verbal defense will work. Spitting, stuttering, and tripping over one's tongue is caused by shallow breathing.

When Verbal Techniques Don't Work

Teach your child to only use physical defense as a last resort, when he can't go to the teacher, walk away, or when his personal control, clever persuasion, and escape techniques are not effective.

If your child is forced into a physical confrontation with a bully, the next step for your child is to create safety space. Encourage your child to maintain at least 6 feet of distance from the bully. This will make it necessary for the bully to make at least two actions in order to physically fight. When it's not possible to be at least 6 feet apart, teach your child to stand with his hands up, not in a threatening or defensive position. He can pretend to be scratching his cheek or brushing back his hair. In case the criminal attempts a sucker punch, your child's hands will be in a better position to block or at least dissipate the blow.

Teach your child to watch for pre-attack postures by the potential assailant. Is he standing as if he is blading—putting one foot in front of the other? Is he shifting his shoulders? Clenching his fists? Teach your child to immediately move his space. Each time your child moves, he is forcing the potential assailant to at least change his thinking about how to attack.

Practice safety space with your child by standing across from each other. Simulate different stances, clenching your fists or shifting your shoulders as if about to attack. Have your child move his space, either backward or to the side. Show your child how this movement of his space forces you to reposition your stance in order to attack. We call this "having happy feet." Keep moving!

If the disrespectful person continues and your child feels he is going to be physically attacked, teach him to shift his weight (move his space), point his hands (palms facing each other) toward the attacker, and demand that he stop. In order for your child to quickly move away from a physical attack, teach him to follow this principle: Whichever direction your child wants to move, move that foot first! If moving backward, move his back foot first, then the front foot. If moving to the left, move his left foot first, then the right foot. If moving to the right, move his right foot first, then the left foot. And if moving forward, move his front foot first, then the back foot. This shuffling of the feet—moving the foot *first* in the direction that your child is going—keeps him in balance, avoiding crossover steps, and is quicker to do.

Practice this movement with your child by facing him, and when you make a jerking gesture toward him, have him move one of the four directions following the "move the foot first in the direction he's going" principle. Your child should follow this principle as long as he moves. Two steps to the right turn into a shuffle: right foot first, then left, then right foot again, then left. By following this principle, your child can maintain his balance more easily, reducing his chances of being knocked to the ground.

Keep Away, Push Away, Thrust Away

Keep in mind: A bully is still just another child, and the odds are your child will not be facing a life-and-death attack. Since this is the case, your child needs different physical defense techniques from the standard BST method. The physical moves in this section are designed to disable a bully rather than harm him. If your child is a victim of bullying, engage him in a conversation about the time to use such a technique, and how the aim is to end the altercation, not to cause any degree of harm. **Teach your child that using a throat strike on a bully is never appropriate.**

If the potential bully continues to violate your child's space, there are three physical methods your child can use to protect his space in fairly harmless ways. Each is based upon the speed in which it is delivered. Teach your children the following variations of motions to protect their space. Precede all of these choices by stepping back.

- *Keep* someone out of your space by extending both arms up and out in front of your body, hands open, wrists bent, fingers pointing upward. Think of this as a stop sign. See "Demand" above.
- *Push* someone out of your space by placing both hands up and in front of your body, just in front of the shoulders, hands open, wrists bent, fingers pointing upward. This motion is similar to the down position of a push-up. A push starts out fast then ends up slow. Use a push when someone isn't respecting your verbal demands to keep his distance and keeps crowding you. If you can't avoid a physical confrontation by walking or running away, a push coupled with a verbal command such as "Stay back!" keeps a bully at a distance to prevent a sudden assault.
- Once you've done all that you can to prevent a physical assault and you feel that you are about to be hit, *thrust* an assailant out of your space by placing your hands and arms in the same position as the push. A thrust starts out slow (dead stop) and is executed

by extending your arms forward as fast as you can, striking the other person's chest with the heels of the palms. This has a physically stunning effect on the assailant, reinforcing your demands to stay out of your space.

If abusive behavior occurs on a repeated basis, consider arming your child with a videophone for evidence. Since most cowards don't like to be caught, the threat of documentation alone could be enough of a deterrent to stop the disrespectful behavior. The phone will also provide your child with immediate access to call for help.

When the Bully Is a Coach, Teacher, or Religious Figure

Bullies aren't always other children. Remind your child about applying BST principles even toward adults who everyone trusts to be moral and ethical—teachers, coaches, religious leaders. In some ways, dealing with people who violate trust is even more challenging than dealing with a stranger.

Tell your child to belly-breathe, protect her space, and use strong verbal commands if her space is invaded. If she cannot escape from a physically abusive adult, convince her that you will stand behind her choice to physically defend herself, if necessary. Truly courageous children will not violate your trust in them. Standing up to an adult who is in a position of power takes tremendous courage.

Quick Action Plan for Fighting Bullies

- Use self-control concepts for courage (antidote to fear)
- Bravely communicate disrespect issues to a responsible adult (teacher, parent, principal) using lean, specific words
- In a conflict:
Maintain a reactionary gap of at least 6 feet

Have happy feet and keep moving
Use strong eye contact and voice control
Ask/tell/demand disrespectful person to stop
Use humor, word salad, or *Dragnet* talk
Escape, if possible

Staying Safe At School

The likelihood of a shooting at your child's school is slim. However, many children still fear the possibility of a school shooting. Rather than debate whether or not a child's fear of a school shooting is rational, recognize that to him it is an issue and, depending upon your level of comfort in discussing this topic, give your child some empowerment lessons in hopes of minimizing his fear. Engage your child in a conversation about how he would handle such a situation, providing him with gentle guidance and BST encouragement. Such discussions will go far to help alleviate any fear he may have from seeing stories on the news.

School Response Plans

Since the school shootings at Columbine, many police departments have developed a policy in which the first four officers to arrive on the scene form their own tactical response team and immediately enter the school with the mission to stop the shooter, even before rendering first aid to any victims. We present this information to you so that you will know the commitment and bravery of law enforcement men and women who are willing to do whatever it takes to save innocent lives. Even so, seconds, then minutes, are going to pass between the time the incident starts until these professionals arrive on the scene.

Check out your children's school's critical incident response plan. If they have one, are the staff and students familiar with it? How often is training conducted for the staff? Does the training include participation with police and fire departments? Fire prevention plans and drills have obviously saved many lives in schools. Your child's school needs to model prevention plans and drills for violence. As parents, take an active role in your child's school board or parent associations. Many police and fire agencies nationwide are now actively assisting schools in developing school response plans. A lot of schools use green/yellow/red drills (based on the same concept we talked about for home safety). The school response is driven by the appropriate action to take, depending on the emergency. Green means get out of the building, whether because of fire, explosion, gas leak, suspicious package, bomb threat, and so on. Red for lockdowns is for abduction, anthrax, armed person, and so on. We've helped school systems design such programs. If you need help on a larger level, check out the Resource section at the back of this book.

If your child's school has a lockdown plan in place, make sure that your child understands the importance of responding immediately to any teacher's or staff member's directions (for example, getting into a classroom, sitting against a wall, and so on).

Many schools have implemented a reporting system where students can anonymously report suspicious behavior. To do this takes courage. Kids who have courageously recognized potential dangers and reported warnings to school officials have thwarted many incidents. With not only the courage but also the skills to back up their courage, your children will be able to handle the reporting and not have to run from doing the right thing.

Your Child's Response Plan

Whether your child's school has a response plan or not, give your child concrete tips on how to take care of herself if there ever would be an incident.

Explain the difference between concealment and cover. Concealment is something that just hides your child and is not necessarily thick enough to prevent bullets from penetrating, for example, drywall, doors, or desks. Cover is something that will protect your children from gunfire: thick concrete or metal, thick trees if outdoors, behind the engine portion of cars with their feet at the wheels, and possibly even compressed paper.

We found that 2.5 to 3.5 inches of compressed paperstacked books or even heavy school bookbags can serve as emergency cover. *We are not guaranteeing that any specific amount of compressed paper will stop all bullets.* The bullet-resistant vests of police officers will not stop all bullets. We only propose the idea as a possible means of hope and empowerment in a desperate situation.

Peace of Mind at School—for You *and* Your Child

Your goal is to allow your child to go to school feeling safe, so she can concentrate on school activities. Your courage coaching will greatly contribute to your child's belief that she can handle school challenges—from bullying to critical incidents—and will give you peace of mind that your child is strong, brave, and prepared.

11

THE FAMILY DEFENSE PLAN OUTSIDE OF HOME AND SCHOOL

As your child gets older, her freedom to be on her own will increase. Her exposure to the larger world will increase, too, along with her risks and responsibilities. However, rather than worrying about your child's increased exposure, focus instead on giving her tools to prepare her for her increased freedom and the belief in herself that she can and will handle ambiguous situations. Teach her that you'll support her doing the best that she can in critical decision-making.

In the following chapters, you'll find specific safety scenarios. Start discussions about these scenarios by putting things into perspective. Fear of the unknown adds to our anxiety. When we believe we can handle a crisis or critical incident, chemicals such as cortisone and noradrenaline energize us. If we don't believe we can handle the situation, these chemicals shut us down. Your goal is to have your child want to, not have to, follow BST strategies to keep safe while enjoying freedom.

Note that some of the following scenarios include tactics to deal with violent acts. Please use your judgment when deciding what to share with your child. Share the information only in the way that you feel best gets the message across to your child based upon her level of maturity. If you feel that a different word or phrase makes some of this information easier for your child to understand, go for it! The bottom line is to give your child realistic hope that she can control, manage, or at least survive a worst-case scenario.

There are many ways that you can practice and/or discuss scenarios with your child, including the role-playing and mental rehearsal we covered earlier. A technique we call "If I Weren't Afraid, I'd ..." is an additional method you can use to activate your child's tactical thinking. While working to build up your younger children's confidence you might get responses from them that they're too afraid to do what you're teaching them. Help them get past their hesitation of taking action by saying, "If I Weren't Afraid, I'd . . . " This statement acknowledges where they are now—frightened—and gets them to the action stage of thinking. By pacing them in this way, you're still getting their critical thinking brain in gear.

Mall Safety

We know kids like to hang out at malls. However, malls can be dangerous places for children on their own. We allowed our children to *shop* at the mall and never hang out there as if it were an amusement park. We created some family mall safety rules, rules that you may want to share with your children.

Never allow young children to go to mall restrooms by themselves. If they are the opposite sex of you and too old to go in your restroom, wait outside the door for them. Allow a reasonable time for them to exit and if you're concerned that something may be wrong, go in anyway and check on your child.

While shopping with your young child, keep sight of each other. Because of his grasp on the BST Family Defense plan, hopefully your child will not fall for cons, tricks, or treats offered by someone to lure him away. Before going to the mall, remind your child about cash for courage.

Teach your children to walk throughout the mall and parking lot with confidence—belly-breathing, gripping, looking around, and being in control of their space. Criminals don't usually attack people who demonstrate that level of spirit and confidence. Tell your child that malls are havens for theft crimes—whether stealing packages from cars or stealing purses. Courage coach your child that if challenged, she must do the best she can to prevent a theft or robbery by using her self-control strategies (belly-breathing, gripping, eye contact, space protection, and verbal skills). Do not fight for property, especially if the attacker is armed. After the criminal leaves, celebrate the fact that your child may have prevented a worse crime because of her self-control.

Preplan what your child will do should he get separated from you or lost in the mall. Recommend that he find a uniformed security or police officer or a woman with kids and tell them he needs help. As a general rule, teach your child to ask a woman rather than a man for help.

Parks

If everyone who wanted to go to the park would go, we'd have safe parks, due strictly to numbers. Unfortunately, too many Americans deny themselves the beauty of parks because of fear. However, with careful planning and BST techniques, you can make the park a safe experience for every member of your family.

When taking your young child to the park, determine the size of space (hula-hoop) you and your child will play in. As with malls, do not allow your child to go to the restroom without you. At the very least, wait just outside the door. Sit within your child's extended space—near the swing set or slide. Acknowledge other people around you with glancing eye contact and if you or your child feel the creeps, leave.

Car Safety

Cars greatly expand your teenager's world. Emphasize to your teenagers that driving a car is a privilege, not a right. There is awesome responsibility that goes with this privilege. Besides the safe operation of a car, obeying speed limits, and other traffic laws, your child may be challenged by unexpected tests while driving—unsafe and discourteous drivers, bad weather, accidents, breakdowns, road rage, and so on. Teach your child the following responses to unexpected situations.

Auto Accident

A child old enough to drive a car needs advanced BST strategies. Teach your child that if she is involved in an auto accident to call the police and you immediately. Tell your child not to discuss who's at fault or admit any guilt to the other driver. If the other driver is upset or angry, have your child stay in her car until the police arrive.

If the accident occurs in a business area, encourage your child to wait inside a business until the police and/or you arrive. If the other driver invades your child's space, teach her to use the Ask/Tell/Demand Principles we discussed in Chapter 10. If the other driver and/or his occupants continue to threaten your child or make her fear for her safety and her car is drivable, tell her it's OK to drive to where there are other people or to the police station if she knows its location. She should then immediately contact the police and report the accident and the threatening behavior. Leaving the scene of an accident for reasonable safety is understandable. Your child is not failing to report the accident. She will do so as soon as safely possible.

Traffic Stop

If your child is being pulled over by the police in an isolated location, and she is afraid because she is not sure it is really a police officer, teach her to put on her flashers and dome light, acknowledge the officer with a wave, and drive to a public place such as a gas station or firehouse. Continuing to drive at reasonable speed and acknowledging to the officer that you are aware he wants you to stop is not considered fleeing or eluding the police. (The safety of the police officer is also important.) Driving to a public place can also be a safety plan if stopped in isolated areas. Once stopped, tell your child to explain her fear to the officer. This is a tactic to be used respectfully, especially when there are reports in your area of assailants posing as police officers to commit crime.

Teach your children how to identify legitimate police officers. Research the color of lights on police cars in your area. There is a nationwide effort to just assign the color blue only to law enforcement vehicles. The switch has not yet been made in all states. Call your local station to ask how police cars in your area are identified.

Uniformed police officers in the United States wear badges and must have a photo ID on them at all times. Professional officers will understand your child's anxiety and will not be offended if your child asks to see the identification of someone who pulls him over. Most importantly, real officers carry police radios that create audio transmissions your children can hear or can request to hear.

Cell Phone

Arm your independent children with a cell phone so they can call for help if their car breaks down or they feel someone in a car is stalking them. In addition to a cell phone, consider putting a large, fluorescent SEND POLICE banner in every car your family owns. You can buy or make a fluorescent SEND POLICE sign that is large enough to be seen by passing cars, approximately 8 × 30 inches. Should your child's car break down, have her call the police and you with her cell phone. In addition, ask her to hang the SEND POLICE banner inside or outside the back window. It's possible that others who see the sign will also call the police. Make sure the sign specifically states SEND POLICE. Do not use banners that say SEND HELP or CALL POLICE. Neither of these messages is a specific command for police to respond.

If there are public places nearby, have your teenager walk to that location using her BST skills. If there is no place within walking distance, have your teenager stay in the car, with her doors and windows locked. If someone stops, teach her to wait until that person walks up to her car. If your teenager has a cell phone and it works, teach her to be on it with the police or you as someone approaches to help.

If your teen has no cell phone, she needs to:

- Belly-breathe, grip the steering wheel, and speak loud enough to be heard through a partially lowered window.
- Say: "Thanks for stopping. You're the second person to stop. A guy left here about 10 minutes ago and has called the police. Would you mind leaving and calling the police again?"

  A decent person will respect your child's request. Teach your child to repeat her request if the person does anything other than leave. If he says, "I'm a mechanic. Let me check your engine," tell your daughter to switch *orange* with the following firm response.

  Say: "No. Leave and call the police again!" No matter what the other person suggests,—a ride, rest in his warm truck, and so on—she is to insist that he leave and call the police again. Your child should never get out of the car! If the other person does not respect her wishes and tries to get inside her car, she should be ready to switch red and apply the T principle of BST.

Road Rage

In police work, cars are sometimes referred to as 2000-pound weapons when their operators drive them criminally or recklessly. Teach your child that the best defense against an erratic driver and his weapon is to get away as quickly as possible.

Tell your child not to engage in any sparring such as horn blowing or hand gestures. If your child accidentally cuts off another driver and the other driver blows his horn or makes an obscene gesture, teach your child to have the self-control to acknowledge his mistake by waving respectfully to the other driver and moving on. If the other driver persists in aggressive behavior, such as tailgating, pulling in front of your child and slamming on the brakes, and so on, tell your child to get away from the stranger's car and call the police. If your child has a cell phone, even if he can't use it while driving, have him at least pretend to be using it to scare the other driver. Review these techniques with your teenage driver anytime your family sees or hears about a road rage incident in the news.

Carjacking

Thieves who steal cars while someone is in the car are called carjackers. Carjackers approach cars stopped at intersections, gas stations, or even in fast food drive-through lanes. Remind your child of B and S skills applicable to driving—belly-breathing, gripping, positive thoughts for safe operation. In addition, encourage your child to scan the area around her car (her space) when she is stopped for a short period of time.

Teach your child that she has your permission to *safely* run red lights or stop signs if she ever feels the creeps because of someone standing on the corner. If a police officer stops her, she can share her concern with the officer. If the officer doesn't understand her, the ticket is worth the price of her safety.

Get your teenage driver in the habit of not stopping too closely behind cars stopped in front of him on the street or in fast food restaurant drive-through lanes. Teach your child to stop back far enough that he can see the license plate of the car in front of him. This will allow your child to maneuver his car around the stopped car in front, if he has the need to do so.

If your child is the victim of a carjacking, have her use her self-control skills of belly-breathing so that she can comply with the carjacker's demand for her to get out of the car. Some carjackers perceive victims who hold their breath as resisting. They are not—they can't move if they're not breathing!

Teach your child to *never* go with the carjacker. If the carjacker demands that your child drive or that your child move over to the passenger seat, teach her to get out and run. Tell your child to *never* allow a criminal to take her from one location to another. Your child has better odds of surviving at point A, where the crime originates, than point B, where the attacker wants to go. The only reason the attacker wants to move your child is because he is afraid of witnesses and the uncontrolled environment of point A. He wants to move your child to point B, a place he knows that is isolated.

Protecting Yourself From Criminals

Your teenager might work in a fast food restaurant or retail store part-time. At the very least, your child is a customer in one of these places. Your child could be the victim of a robbery while working in or patronizing a store.

Most robbers threaten that they have a weapon. If the gun or knife is only being used as a threat, teach your child not to resist. Calmly, engaging in belly-breathing, your child should give up property to a robber. As long as the gunman is only interested in stealing property, calm (belly-breathing) compliance is the best response.

However, some criminals use guns or knives as weapons to attack someone. In these situations, if escape is not possible, your child must improve his chances of survival by learning how to protect himself against a weapon. See Chapter 12 for how to teach your child to defend against a gun or knife being used as a weapon.

Put a Handle on Your Child's Keys

Just like gripping a steering wheel in a car for self-control, putting a handle on your child's keys allows your child to have something to grip in a threatening situation. As we mentioned in earlier chapters, an item about the size of a Magic Marker or permanent marker is ideal for gripping—consider using a mini-wrench, a mini-flashlight, or a Kubotan (a 5½-inch mini-baton). Find something that is virtually unbreakable so that your child's keys don't fly all over the place if they have to strike someone. Also, make sure the grip item is long enough to protrude out of both sides of your child's grip.

By gripping the handle on his keys, your child's blood is circulating by default—enhancing his self-control. His confidence is displayed through this self-control with belly-breathing, gripping, eye contact, and space control. Self-confident body language alone may be enough to deter a criminal from targeting your child.

In a physical attack, either end of a key-chain handle can be thrust into the attacker's throat. Flight attendants that we've trained became very empowered when we shared this concept with them. They are mandated to carry a mini-flashlight while on duty. They didn't realize the self-control and self-defense power of this gripper until we showed them how to use it.

Other Self-Defense Products

Other than putting a handle on your keys, mostly to improve self-control blood circulation, we believe most self-defense products are "maybe" products. Yes, they can be effective but they can also work against you in threatening situations: sprays may be outdated, and whistles or alarms may not attract help. As police officers, we responded many times with lights and sirens, and drug-crazed assailants weren't scared away. Police officers use chemical sprays for control and yet often the spray fails to stop an enraged, intoxicated criminal. We believe your child can protect himself better by empowering himself with personal belief in his ability to use verbal skills to talk down most violence, protect his space, escape if possible, and in a worst-case scenario, cause injury to an attacker, and survive weapon attacks.

If you still want your child to have a self-defense product (shriek alarm, chemical irritant, and so on), at the very least, teach her not to have total dependence on the product for protection. Teach her that if the product fails to have the desired effect on the attacker, she should then use the canister or product container to strike the attacker's throat.

Win and Come Home!

Your child's ability to handle an unexpected critical incident, especially an armed attack, comes from her belief that she can handle worst-case situations. Teaching your child under conditions of moderate, controlled adversity will train her mind that she has already been through this before and has survived. Convince her she has the personal skills necessary to win and come home!

12

THE FAMILY DEFENSE PLAN AGAINST WEAPONS

The topics covered in this chapter are serious—thinking about your child confronting a criminal with a weapon is a frightening prospect. However, our goal in this chapter is to teach you how to instill a foundation of memorable principles that your golden children can use, along with red BST choices, that will greatly improve your children's odds of surviving an armed attacker. Please read this material carefully; then reread it to ensure that you fully understand the principles needed to empower your children to survive an attack involving a weapon.

We offer no guarantees—they do not exist—for our children or yours. However, our principles do offer a way to improve your child's odds, because these survival odds are not acceptable:

Armed Attacker's Odds = 100%   Your Children's Odds = 0%

Even with the guidance presented in this book, it is important to accept this reality. If an attacker is armed and your child is not, the odds will never be equal at 50/50. That is unrealistic. Our goal is to increase your children's odds in the hopeful range between 1 to 49 percent, which is better than nothing. Your children's maturity, self-control, and application of BST blended with these weapon survival principals and luck will determine where this number falls.

From this point on, we are going to offer clear, concise principles that you can teach your children. Principles such as $2 \times 2 = 4$ are consistent, whether multiplying 20×20 or 200×200. The math may get complicated; however accurate, simple principles lead the student to the answer. We believe the same concept is true when teaching weapon survival—simple principles that your children understand can lead them to answers that significantly improve their odds to live.

Start by preparing your children with this fact: The sight of a weapon in an attacker's hand is going to take your breath away! While fighting for air, your children rapidly need to figure out if the attacker is using that gun/knife/bottle/brick as a threat (to get what he wants) or as a weapon (to cause injury or death).

Assessing Risk

When a robber aims a gun at a store clerk and says, "Give me the money or I will shoot," the gun is being used as a threat to get money. If the armed robber gets mad because there is not enough money/things—and escalates the crime by grabbing the clerk—the gun then becomes a weapon, meant to cause injury.

If an attacker walks into the store, walks right past the cash register, shoots his gun, then pushes the clerk in a back storage room, it is obvious that this criminal is using the gun from the start as a weapon to injure or kill. At this point, the clerk has nothing to lose by attempting to defend herself against that weapon. The problem is, most golden people have no specific idea of what to do in such a scenario. The good news is, whether your child is a customer or working in the store, she will have strategies to call upon because of your investment of time in teaching this material.

If your children ever face an armed attacker, prepare them to understand that their body is going to go into major alarm mode. Their initial need is twofold. They need to control themselves and figure out rapidly what the attacker wants. Here are the words to use for guidance:

1. Breathe, grip your hands, visualize loved ones (self-control)
2. Talk: "What do you want?" (What is the attacker's goal?)

It is critical that your children figure out what the armed attacker's goals are—as quickly as possible. What criminals want falls into three simple categories:

Property   Desire for things: money, car, purse, and so on
Body   Desire for physical or sexual assault
Life   Desire to kill

Property

If the armed attacker wants property, teach your children to give up property. Teach the phrase: "think like a bank!" Of course, it is upsetting to just give items up—banks don't like it at all. However, resistance to robbery can escalate the attacker's desire for money to a desire to hurt people. That probability of escalation is not worth the risk in most cases. As a general principle, teach your children not to fight for their property physically, especially if an attacker is armed.

Body

If an armed attacker does not want your child's things, or has already taken things, and force continues, it is critical that your child continue to work toward self-control with breathing, gripping, and visualizing loved ones. If a criminal is preparing to attack your child sexually, there are three potential responses: (1) Pretend to comply in an effort to stall for time and better figure out what to do; (2) comply/submit to sexual assault, or (3) fight against sexual assault. Here is how to explain this to your child.

Pretend to Comply

Do all in your power to slow things down. Keep talking. Ask things like "What do you want? Stop. Talk to me. I'll help you. Slow down. Wait …". The more you slow down the violence, the more luck you are adding to the equation. Maybe a witness will appear. Maybe the assailant will calm down. If he gets scared or angry and escalation erupts, look for your opportunity to defend yourself physically. (We'll explain how to defend against weapons later in this chapter.)

Comply

The goal in violence is to save your life! If sacrificing your body to sexual assault is needed to save your life, then your choice is honorable. No one has the right to second-guess your intentions, feelings, reasons, and choices.

Although the armed criminal has temporary control of your body, he will never have control of your mind. Think to yourself, *You have me now, I'll have you later in court!* Breathe deeply and memorize as many details as you can. Gather evidence as a way to regain control during an event that is out of your control. Touch, take, and leave as much physical evidence as you can to help detectives later catch and convict this person.

Take: His hair (pinched out by the roots for accurate DNA readings) from his head, arms, hands, knuckles. Take fibers from his sweater, shirt, or coat; take buttons; and claw his body to get skin under your nails. Claw the ground, grab grass, grab carpet fiber, and so on. Keep from losing these small items by placing them in a pocket, down in your clothing—and especially in your mouth. Yes, it's scary to think about; however, emergency room professionals will compliment you for your brilliant planning and courage as valuable evidence is collected from your body and given to the police to build your case.

Leave: Your hair (pinched out by the roots for accurate DNA readings) from your head or arms, hands, and knuckles. Leave fiber from your clothing, broken fingernails, buttons, jewelry, and shoes. Put these items on the attacker, especially down in his pockets. Also leave this evidence all over the environment where the attack is occurring.

Touch: In addition to the deliberate exchange of evidence, touch as many smooth surfaces as you can to leave your fingerprints. Scratch messages in the dirt or on the seat of a car with your fingernails. Write by clawing important data, like a license number or name, on your arm.

This deliberate exchange of evidence gives survivors tremendous credibility and power, as it provides police with the evidence they need to prove that an attack occurred and to catch the attacker.

After an assault occurs, an armed attacker makes one of two choices. The survivor is either released or killed. If the attacker intends on releasing you, you will know it because he will tell you or just do it. If the attacker is quiet (especially if a car is involved and he keeps driving you around), you need to prepare to physically fight and defend yourself.

Fight

If an armed attacker approaches you with the intention to assault you and you are breathing calmly and confidently, not frozen by fear, you have the right to physically defend yourself to save your life.

How to Defend Against an Armed Attacker

Courage Coaches, hang in there. It is reasonable to be uncomfortable with the thought of having these discussions with your children. The material is red and your family is golden! Keep reminding yourself that if you don't teach your children these life-saving principles, odds are no one else will. Your goal is to give them red options to improve their odds against an armed red attacker. An effective fight requires golden people to switch to their attacker's red color plus 1 percent!

Life

We have spent over 30 years researching and training in defensive tactics for civilian and law enforcement audiences. We are convinced that when civilians, especially children, choose to defend themselves (before or after rape, or during a physical attack) they need one additional physical choice to add to their BST Family Defense.

In the split seconds of being faced with a violent person intending on using a weapon, your children cannot sort through a laundry list of tactics specific to a particular weapon. Your children cannot be expected to instantly retain and recall a set of weapon-specific strategies. Your children can, however, learn and remember one principle-based weapon defense strategy that will greatly increase their odds for survival. The summary word for that principle is *grab*. Teach your children to grab with their hand(s) the most dangerous part of any weapon in order to protect their critical zone.

Critical Zone Protection

The head, neck, and torso (the chest and stomach) are the most critical parts of the human body. We refer to this area of the body as the kill zone. You may want to make that term more child-friendly by calling it the critical zone. Whatever you decide to call it, know that the area is important because protection of that zone is a matter of life or death.

Our experience has taught us that weapon-wielding attackers do not attack in slow-motion using predictable moves. Weapon attacks are quick with unpredictable motion. In order to defend their life, your children must be willing to sacrifice injury to their limbs (hands, arms, legs, and feet) to protect against injury to their critical zone. Injuries to limbs are not usually life-threatening; injuries to organs in the critical zone usually are.

Grab Defense

We recommend that you teach your children to initially respond to an armed attacker by throwing back their arms into the universally understood "I give up" position (a standing push-up position) while they decide what to do. If fighting is their choice, they must then grab the most dangerous part of the weapon aimed at them. By grabbing the weapon they, not the criminal, decide which part of their body is going to be injured.

To improve odds of surviving, help your children understand that it is better to be hurt in the hand rather than in the heart, neck, or head. Consider teaching your children to grab specific parts of various weapons this way:

Grab guns by the barrel. When you move the barrel, you are moving the bullets. It is not our recommendation that you try to out-muscle the armed attacker in an attempt to take his gun away. That kind of action involves too much wild movement of the gun barrel. Our recommendation to minimize injury is to move the barrel one direction—up, down, or to the side—so that if bullets are fired, they strike less critical parts of your body and/or your hand(s). Be willing to accept that your hand(s) are going to be injured, in addition to bodily injury outside of your critical zone. Once you have moved the gun, hit the attacker's throat and run.

This heroic response is already instinctively inside you. If you saw someone point a gun at a family member's head, you would intuitively see why it is necessary to risk injury to your hand(s) in order to move bullets away from her critical head area, then fight the attacker (which you now know means strike the throat).

Grab knives by the blade. While most parents preach do not touch the blade to their children for safety, for crime survival we want you to teach the opposite: "Grab the blade"—to save your life! This choice is a last resort. As long as a blade is cutting your hand(s), it cannot cut any part of your critical zone. This courageous choice gives you a chance to control what area of your body is cut or stabbed. Use two hands at first if that is what it takes to stop, block, and grab the blade from getting near your critical zone. Make sure at least one hand keeps a tight grip on the blade as your other hand struggles to strike the attacker's throat to end the attack. Never try to wrestle the knife away: Your goal is to grab it to protect your critical zone, then stop the attack with a strike to the throat.

Your hand(s) will get cut. A tight grip on the blade will reduce the blade's movements and reduce injury; likewise, a loose grip allows more movement and more injury. Knife injuries to hand(s) and arm(s) aren't usually life threatening. Knife injuries to organs in the critical zone can be life-threatening.

Grab other weapons. The grab weapon survival principle provides one courageous yet instinctive response for most types of weapons used by armed attackers:

Grab and redirect a bottle (intact or broken)
Grab and redirect a hammer
Grab and redirect a screwdriver
Grab and redirect a baseball bat

Quick Guide to Weapon Defense

In summary, we offer this complete set of principles for you to teach your children to consider when facing an armed attacker:

1. Belly-breathe, grip your hands, visualize loved ones (Self-control)
2. Talk: "What do you want?"
3. Respond to what the armed attacker wants:
   Things—Give up property
   Body—Pretend to comply, comply, or fight against rape
   Life—Defend your life by fighting
4. Grab weapon tightly, direct it to the side, up or down away from critical zone
5. Hit the throat
6. Run

You can practice these weapon defense choices with your mature children two ways: mentally and physically.

Mental Rehearsals for Gun Defenses

Hollywood provides an enormous amount of mental practice opportunities for your family; you can turn entertainment into covert courage coaching lessons. Make it a habit to humorously critique the unrealistic and inaccurate fight scenes depicted in violent movies and on TV shows. Remember, the lessons need to be short sound bite comments, not lengthy conversations. When fight scenes are done right, cheer enthusiastically; when they are done poorly, suggest corrections based on our BST Family Defense plan. (Obviously, in theaters you need to hold back your verbal critiques of violent scenes, good or bad, until the drive home—or you take a chance of being asked to leave the theater!)

Physically Practicing Gun Defenses

When watching movies and TV shows at home that depict unrealistic fight scenes, hit the pause button on the VCR or DVD and reenact the scenes, allowing your children to grab and redirect finger-guns as they playfully move toward the pretend attacker's throat with their other hand. (Remember, absolutely *no* strikes or touches to the throat when practicing!) The movie creates the energy of suspense, so in that excited state, have your children repeat the movie scene with life-saving improvements. Include theatrical roar noises as much as possible. Keep these critiques fun and short, with no lectures, only gentle instruction and enthusiastic encouragement. Our kids love watching movies with us, and so do their friends. It's fun to turn entertainment with rented movies and popcorn into regular courage coaching sessions!

As an outdoor activity, use squirt guns as an even more dramatic way to practice gun defenses. After you explain the principle, let your child be the bad guy first! Then reverse roles. Encourage your child to shove the water gun up against different parts of your body, See if you can turn quickly enough that the water shoots past your critical zone, then gently make a motion toward your child's throat. This type of physical practice creates muscle memory and allows your children to see how logical the response is and also feel how fast and effective the grab technique can be. Your goal is not development of perfect technique. Your goal is development of perfect belief in the technique so that if they are ever desperate, muscle memory joins their mental Courage Command from you: "I will find a way to save myself—for the love of my family."

Note: Practice the movements needed to make slow strikes toward the throat with your child. Real strikes to the throat at any speed are never allowed because they work! **Never let children practice these motions with each other, just with their Courage Coach.**

Do you want to test your children's ability to think through a complicated scenario on their own? Practice a surprise attack scenario by putting a squirt gun in the center of your child's back. Your child will quickly realize that guns in the back are dangerous because it is hard to accurately grab the barrel in that situation. Encourage your child to react by acting afraid before the grab. By throwing her arms back into the "I give up" position as she squirms into a partial turn, she'll learn she can better see and grab the gun barrel with accuracy. A few seconds of acting afraid will likely be tolerated by an armed attacker—an attacker who does not realize it is a performance created with the intention of improving body positioning. What you and your children will learn from practicing this kind of attack and response is that even if a shot of water is fired, it will probably miss your critical zone.

Mental Rehearsals for Knife Defenses

For mental rehearsals of knife defense, we again recommend using movies and/or news footage as prompts to think through the BST possible choices that might involve grabbing knives by the blade. Mental rehearsals are a good time to remind your children that although their hands will be injured, they are not likely to feel excessive pain from cuts during their defensive fighting because of shock, which is the temporary inside chemical changes that protect a body during a crisis. Injuries will hurt more later.

Also, watch carefully and discuss with your children the extent that actors and actresses will go to dramatize the freeze response in crimes. Acting (especially exaggerated soap opera–type acting) provides a wonderful study of how most victims respond, especially at the sight of knives in violence—but not *your* children!

Physical Practice for Knife Defense

Start with toy rubber knives or dull plastic knives. Ask your children to gently hold those knives in their hands and get comfortable while breaking the old rule to not touch a knife by the blade. Next put duct tape around the blade of a dull dinner knife and ask your child to grab it by the blade as you start to pull on it from the handle, creating resistance. This practice looks like tug-of-war! Never try to wrestle a knife away—what you are trying to teach your children is that they can grab and hold on to a moving knife blade. Now, try this action a third time, having your child try to quickly grab the protected blade (make it hard for them to catch) and then to follow up with a pretend movement toward your throat.

The tighter your child grabs the knife, the less it will move in his hand, and the less it will cut his hand. However, avoiding a cut completely is not likely. By contrast, a loose grip will allow the blade to move more and cut more. Have your child drop the fabric from his long sleeve (or coat) over his hand, creating the possibility of physical protection to reduce injury. Picking up a magazine or any other physical object to use as a shield to prevent a knife attack also provides protection until the throat can be struck.

Consider practicing knife defense techniques with your teenagers, using colored markers and old sweatshirts! Take turns being good guys/bad guys to test the ability to grab the marker before it strikes the torso. Your teens will know when they missed because their hands and sweatshirt will show pretend injury locations. Do this with great animation and fun. We do not believe in scaring children; we believe in empowering them to believe they can at least try! As a Courage Coach, your goal is not to perfect the knife defense technique. Your goal is to perfect belief in the principle of the technique—injure my hands and arms but save my critical zone!

Protecting Airways

Your child's air (oxygen) is the most important element to protect in a sudden attack. Your child's survival in a strangulation or smothering event depends on her immediate fight for air. Make sure your child is armed with your lifesaving Courage Command to help her stay emotionally strong during the critical, initial seconds of her sudden airless state—I can do it!

Criminals will use just about anything as a strangulation weapon—rope, wire, panty hose, coat hangers, electric cord, guitar string, and so on. Remind your child that the space behind her is the most vulnerable to sudden attack. Therefore, when walking, she needs to walk as if she were the queen, constantly turning her head and confronting any noise from behind. If a strangulation attack occurs, teach this response explanation summarized by these words: *Turn around and fight.* Consider teaching this technique to your children in the following way.

It is a natural response to try to get your fingers under that strangulation tool to pull it off your neck. *Do not touch the strangulation weapon.*

Touching or grabbing adds to the pressure of the choke and, even worse, it ties up your hands which you need to fight! Instead, turn around as quickly as possible to relieve the strangulation tool's pressure from the front of your neck. By turning, no matter how difficult (even if you have to fall to the ground), you are likely to have loosened the strangulation tool from against the front of your throat to the back of your neck. This happens because the attacker's arms and body are forced to shift as you shift. Your goal is to find air, any way you can. Turning to face the attacker also gives you improved position to strike his throat and run!

Practice Air Recovery

Mental rehearsals while watching movies and TV are best for young children. However, we recommend physically practicing this response to strangulation attacks with your teenagers, especially if they are college-bound. From behind, gently place a soft, wide belt (terry cloth robe belts are perfect) around your teenager's neck. No force is needed. Have him turn around rapidly to face you so he can feel how turning immediately took the pressure off his throat (actually the entire front neck area). Have him gently make a strike motion toward your throat to complete the muscle memory response you want him to have in a strangulation scenario.

You can also practice this strangulation response with your teenager in the car. Even though the steering wheel and seat headrest create a challenge in turning, your teenager can still turn his neck and shoulders enough to release pressure so he can breathe and reach back to strike the attacker's throat. Repeat to your teenager that strangulation attacks create a battle for air. Fight to keep your air while stopping the criminal's air.

Because this is the only nongrab weapon response, repeat this summary to your teenagers:

1. Turn immediately toward the attacker.
2. Strike the throat.
3. Run!

Protecting the Power of One

When you are faced with multiple attackers, as with any scenario, safe escape is always the best choice. Because multiple attackers can be a frightening concept, we recommend you discuss this topic with your children starting in their teenaged years. It is hard to escape this kind of attack, but you can provide your teenagers with these options to consider:

1. Breathe, grip, and visualize loved ones (Self-control)
2. Dial 9-1-1. (Give location and do not hang up.)
3. Ask, "What do you want?" (Give up things if you can accommodate.)
4. Move your space in clever ways to protect your body, shouting "Call Police!"
5. Fight!

Teach these space examples to your children: Create unexpected behavior by using dramatic theatrics such as turning immediately and walking into moving traffic (carefully, of course!). Walk down the middle line of the street, allowing all those who are honking—to become witnesses. Creating this type of commotion forces attackers to change their game plan. Hopefully, their choice is to go away.

In an isolated area where no witnesses exist, call 9-1-1 on your cell phone. Give your location first. Keep gripping your phone with 9-1-1 on line, to record the entire event, even if you are not talking to them. Using red language, shout verbal commands to get away. Position your back against a wall or any physical barrier as you walk to prevent one of the attackers from attacking you from behind.

Keep your eyes moving from one attacker to the other throughout. Keep looking for clever escape routes and/or witnesses to appear. If you see someone, yell out "Call police!" If an unstoppable attack occurs, roar and fight efficiently—one throat at a time! Use your phone or your hand as a weapon. The alternative choice, doing nothing, is not likely to help. The good news is that multiple-attacker crimes occur far less than one-on-one crimes where your odds of survival are greatly increased.

Quick Guide to Weapon Survival

Your children's ability to handle an unexpected critical incident, especially an armed attack, comes from their belief that they can handle worst-case situations, because in playful situations, they have been through it before. Encourage your children to think through and develop muscle memory by acting out weapon defense scenarios, especially when in the state of emotional stimulation caused by a frightening scene in a movie or TV show, which gives your children an edge. Armed with a courageous mind-set and the BST Family Defense skills, you—their Courage Coach—have prepared them to face fear and adversity with this powerful belief: I've been through this before; I can do it! Your courage and willingness to teach your children courageous weapon survival principles will greatly increase their odds of survival from somewhere between 1 to 49 percent—and that is so much better than the odds of disbelievers— zero!

13

THE BST WAY TO COMMUNICATE

Parenting has always been a challenging job. Today the job is more difficult than ever. We commend you for your personal discipline and willingness to be your children's Courage Coach. Preparing your children with the courage and self-control needed to face your and their worst fears is the best way to manage or at least survive an unanticipated and critical incident.

When your children are taught to believe *I can find a way* to handle the worst-case scenarios we've talked about, then lesser everyday challenges become even easier. Empowerment is the opposite of despair. Empowered (courageous) children approach situations, good and bad, with optimism, because it is the language they most know! Work on making this language part of your everyday family life by creating a courage vocabulary—a language of love that empowers your children to make brave, smart decisions.

Courage Vocabulary

Do your children say these four-letter words every day: love, care, give, hope, help, kind? The daily use of golden words creates a natural repellant against daily, careless usage of red four-letter words that you know your children hear several times a day: hate, punk, jerk, @#$%, and so on.

We encourage your family to use the following words regularly (hopefully as earned compliments) for the development of optimism, self-control, and safety:

Brave	Fearless	Strong	Sincere
Courageous	Awesome	Moral	Creative
Noble	Righteous	Incredible	Humble
Spectacular	Proud	Inspiring	Responsible
Loyal	Punctual	Strategic	Visionary
Respectful	Tenacious	Curious	Generous

After speaking at a business conference, an attorney waited with his wife to speak to us privately, concerned about the safety of their three daughters, ages 8 to 15. He wanted to know when to start teaching the BST Family Defense plan, and of course we said, now! We asked him how many times a month he used the word *courage* in a conversation with his daughters. He looked at his wife, shook his head, and said, "Never." We respectfully asked him, "How can you expect your daughters to have a character trait that powerful, if you rarely or never use the word in your home?" He genuinely responded, "I guess we just never thought about it...." Make *courage* an active word in your family.

Adjust Negative Conditioning Phrases

Encourage your family to speak about what *is* instead of what *isn't* going right with your life. Consider these changes in your family dialogue for courage and confidence, in good times and in bad times:

REPLACE	SAY
I can't complain.	I feel good!
I don't disagree.	I agree!
I don't see why not.	Let's do it!
No problem.	It's a pleasure!
That's not bad.	That's good!
That's not what I am saying.	Here is what I am saying.

Don't strike out.	Get a hit!
Don't get upset.	Breathe! Grip! Think positive!
I have to	I'd like to
I'll try to	I will
Problem	Challenge
I failed	I learned
If I only had	Starting now, I will

There are a few other negative words that have become our family's pet peeves. We would like to bring them to your attention, because in dialogue, correction of these two words can diffuse escalation of arguments.

Stop "Shoulding," Please!

Should is a judgment word rooted in blame and guilt. *Should* causes invisible hurt. It is a needless word. Get rid of it. Replace the word *should* with the word *need! Need* is a wonderful replacement word that does not change the meaning of the sentence, except to remove the judgment and guilt. People like to fulfill *needs,* they do not like to fulfill *shoulds.*

You *should* call me when you get there.	You *need* to call me when you get there.
You *should* clean your room right now.	You *need* to clean your room right now.
You *should* have better sense when alone.	You *need* better sense when alone.
You *should* go.	You *need* to go.

To the best of our knowledge the word *should* is not used anywhere in this book, on purpose! We felt no reason to *should* you when giving our advice. It's not your fault that you did not know what we teach, until we teach it! In contrast, the word *need* is used hundreds of times in this book because there are many things we believe you *need* to teach your children as their Courage Coach.

"But" Never Again

Our second pet-peeve word that we rarely use in dialogue is the word *but!* The word *but* is actually a verbal eraser or verbal Delete key! When you construct a phrase, and then pause and say the word *but,* the listener thinks to him- or herself *oh no, here it comes,* and that opening phrase is about to get erased by the phrase following the *but!* We recommend using the replacement word (conjunction) *and!*

She is a good student in school, *but* soccer takes up a lot of her study time.	She is a good student in school, *and* soccer takes up a lot of her study time.
I know you apologized, *but* I didn't like how you were talking to me.	I know you apologized, *and* I didn't like how you were talking to me.
I hear you, *but* you are wrong.	I hear you, *and* you are wrong.

Words create feelings and feelings create behavior! Bad behavior is usually linked to the use of bad words. Good behavior is usually linked to the use of good words. Be careful what you say to the hearts of children you are molding. Just like quality ingredients create fabulous food, quality words create fabulous, courageous, and safe children!

Dependent or Independent?

When your older children ask for favors even though they can perform these tasks themselves, we believe they need to be given this response: "Sure I can make your bed (pick up your toys, get your ice cream, iron your shirt). However, if I do that, does my choice help you to be dependent or independent?" Of course your child will answer *dependent.* Then you say, "Correct. As your parent, it is my job to prepare you to take care of yourself when you live away from home. So, because I love you and your need to prepare for independence, I am going to allow you to make your own bed. Isn't that great! I know you love your independence on Friday night when you want to go skating!"

Using that logic, you will find that your older children, especially your teenagers, will learn to wean off of your maidlike kindness and learn everyday living skills you know they need for survival in college. Please do not wait until the summer before college to think you can teach independence! This independence will translate into the courageous attitude of "I can take care of myself!"

Discussion versus Lecture

In previous chapters, we recommended paying your children cash for courage. This is a technique to reinforce the courage you want your children to display, especially while they are making quality eye contact, voice control, and space protection choices when afraid (whether ordering food at restaurants or talking at an office party with a co-worker, and so on).

Don't Break the Bank

The amount of cash you pay your children needs to be reasonable based on your ability. Please do not think we fill our children's pockets with excessive cash. That is not true. They use money earned from chores and courage to pay for *most* of the extras in their life. The money we save by not *giving* our children cash for extra clothes, pizza, movies, and so on, is the money we use when they *earn* that cash from courage for their extras.

We want to suggest a final twist on cash for courage. When your children, any age, come home and tell you about a challenging event that they conquered with courage (saying "no" to cigarettes, alcohol or drugs, emergency braking to avoid hitting a deer in the road) or an inside story about dangerous choices other kids are making, create this new pattern of response.

1. Listen carefully, nodding your head only. Do not interrupt.
2. Keep quiet. (No comments, no discussion, no lecture … it's hard)
3. When your child is finished, say, *Wow! Your courage deserves a trip to the wallet.* What that comment means is that your child is allowed

to take the single largest bill you have in your wallet as a reward for telling you about something that went wrong that they corrected and what's troubling them—about their friend's bad and dangerous choices.

The purpose of this new pattern of communication is not to over-praise simple accomplishments or reward idle gossip; rather, it is to cele-brate and reward significant acts of courage rooted in quality decision making. Teach your children through cash rewards that they can come home and tell you anything about anything, anyone, anytime. Your new behavior assures them of these promises:

I will not interrupt you.

I will not comment or lecture or (gossip to other parents).

I will pay you for the courage you have demonstrated by *not* partic-ipating in that bad behavior and for your courage to come home and tell me about it.

If the story told to you by your child needs to be addressed, wait until the next day to talk about it again with your child. Bring the topic up casually: "Remember when you told me yesterday about Beth sneaking out of the Jones's house during the sleepover? Well, I'm wondering if you think there is something I need to do because that is risky behavior?"

When you talk to your children like this the next day, your children consider the talk a discussion and they are likely to open up and con-tinue to talk. (Besides, you paid them! They are happy. Who knows, it might happen again!)

If you say that exact comment immediately following your child's disclosure, she'll consider your comment a lecture. We believe children want to talk about the bad choices their friends are making and other difficult decisions they need to make in their life. What they don't want is a lecture format loaded with judgment comments (for example, "That's why I don't like you to spend the night at the Jones's with those girls."). Years of developing your children's trust in this way has tremen-dous impact when your children find themselves in *big* challenges with peer pressure. Knowing they can get out, unload on you, make cash, and talk about it in a reasonable tone later is a dream communication arrangement for your kids and you!

Trust Pays Off for Our Daughter

This pattern of trust worked well for our family years ago when our daughter decided—after 48 hours—to come home from her high school spring break vacation where she shared a house with seven other seniors. Bad things happened. Instead of being a part of it or a witness to it, she trusted she could come home immediately without hearing *"we told you so."* To her delight, her reward was $100. Compared to the danger she walked away from, we felt she deserved much more than that; however, that is the most we could afford for the courage she demonstrated by leaving her vacation!

Her friends—and later, their parents—were stunned by her choice. Instead of placing blame, we suggested to those curious parents that they ask their own children what happened. We were exceedingly proud of our daughter's choice to step away from peer pressure, stay golden, and leave a *red* environment. It is not easy for kids to do the right thing. Consequences are bittersweet. In our daughter's case, she lost a few marginal friends, and most sadly, lost respect for a few close friends who later apologized and worked hard to regain her trust

Always remember, Courage Coach, that when your courageous kids walk away from danger, they do not deserve an *I told you so* lecture, instead they deserve an *I'm so proud of you* celebration!

Sharing Close Calls

Develop a nonpunitive way for your young children to share close calls with you without the fear of being punished. If your children are afraid to tell you about an incident for fear that they will be punished, they won't be able to learn from their mistake and therefore may repeat it.

Develop a ritual whereby your young child can share something with you without fear of judgment. Maybe it's a special chair or a special room where you can debrief an incident with the promise of no punishment.

Consider allowing smaller children to have an elevated position that allows their head to be higher than yours (put them on a stool or on the kitchen counter). This gives them higher status like a judge in a court-room. Encourage your child to tell you his mistakes without your passing judgment. If his behavior requires a lengthy discussion, ask if the child wants to talk about it right then or tomorrow. Honor his request. Then celebrate his courage to talk about his discomfort with thoughts and feelings that he has had or actions he is not proud of.

Debrief to Learn—Like the Pros

Athletes and coaches often watch films after a win or loss of a big sports game, reviewing what went right and wrong, and what needs to change for the next game. Likewise, debriefings are important in other areas of life for learning and growing. Military professionals involved in any incident can debrief without regard to rank or fear of punishment. Firefighters share close calls on a national Internet Web site that protects their identity. The debriefing process allows people in high-risk professions to process their feelings and close calls without punishment. If there is always punishment for making an error or almost making an error, no one could ever learn from their mistakes or from the mistakes of others.

Make it a valued and comfortable habit to debrief your children on challenges they face in life (test taking, party going, driving in a storm, and so on). What you and your children learn together will be insightful and inspiring.

Please do not allow the fear of punishment to keep your children from debriefing with you. The "wait-a-day" rule to create a discussion also allows the Courage Coach extra time, too, to think through new ideas for improved behavior the *next time!*

Sharing the Language of Belief with Your Daughters

Consider this long-time dilemma: Both male and female students, after 4 to 8 years of high school and/or college, graduate and compete for *equal* jobs and *equal* pay that involves *equal* risks—travel, airports, strangers, darkness, parking lots, late working hours, elevators, cab rides, and so on. Who will be better prepared *really* to face risk as a successful graduate in the adult work force? Who received the most encouragement and words of confidence and who had the most freedom during their formidable young adult years? Who, at age 22, is safer? Daughters or sons?

Many parents talk about safety with their teenaged daughters differently than with their teenaged sons. Daughters are traditionally programmed with language emphasizing limitations and the "fear of everything," because as a young woman a daughter is told:

> You are too trusting!
> You are too sweet!
> You are so much smaller!
> Girls are just more vulnerable!
> You are so naïve!
> You always think it is going to happen to someone else!

Sons are traditionally programmed with the language of freedom and the assumption that they can handle anything:

> Just do it!
> Just use your head!
> Get out of there!
> You'll handle it!
> Make it happen!
> Take good care of her!

The discrepancy in this programming is subtle and damaging. Too often young women start their adult lives on a foundation rooted in safety weakness, which can become like quicksand as they develop the fear of taking risks, walking in dark parking lots after working late hours, traveling alone, and so on. By contrast, young men have a better chance to start their adult lives on a foundation rooted in safety strength, which leads to a concrete life where risks are taken regularly and the risks are rewarded. Be aware of these discrepancies, and work to overcome them when working with your own children.

Believe in your sons' and your daughters' natural courage and skills to apply the BST Family Defense equally—empower all your children with the strength they deserve.

Courage Party

Consider throwing a Courage Party with a cake and gifts, if your children survive a difficult challenge that involves extreme courage. We believe that gifts of celebration repel self-doubt or hidden guilt. When children believe that they did the best they could, are recognized by a room full of people they respect, and receive meaningful gifts they will use for years, they are not likely to excessively suffer a lifetime of second-guessing their actions. The gift of *hero* status helps survivors realize that their courage was truly magnificent—they lived!

Our conscious mind cannot accept being both right *and* wrong over the same single event. When families celebrate the actions of a child who has a broken, scared, or suffering heart with a Courage Party, that child is *loved* into releasing any hidden guilt or self-doubt that might remain. The spirit of celebration is more than just gifts for children who have survived a crisis; it is the realization that their life is priceless and cherished! Let your children know that you love them through celebrations of their daily and lifetime courage.

PARTING WORDS
A Lifetime Celebration
of Courage

Legitimate safety is not a short-term service or a product that you can buy *for* your children. It is a long-term investment of time and wisdom that is built *inside* children. We call it backbone. Courage is what builds your children's foundation and makes it strong for a lifetime of quality crisis decision-making. Building this courage starts in early childhood when they need to be positioned on a foundation of high character. The "I'll find a way" spirit radiates inside and outside of children who have the benefit of a strong foundation. This strong foundation is the secret that allows children to be golden, helpful, disciplined, and fun, yet "switch" as needed to deadly serious orange and red behavior on command—to save their lives. Children raised with courage enter adult life with balance and happiness, a direct by-product of learning to keep fear in perspective. All of these qualities can exist in your children, because you have made a decision to build their courage as their Courage Coach.

Personal safety can be a frustrating subject. We live in a society that wants to see, measure, or create a poll that gives everyone proof and validation before they take action, but it is nearly impossible to see the positive effects of a strong courage foundation. Character traits needed for courage involve behaviors and disciplines whose effects cannot be measured for years in the future. Courage stops safety problems before they start because courageous children have the self-control and practiced discipline to notice things or people who seem wrong. We make you this promise: If you work on the development of high character blended with teaching the BST Family Defense, your children will become safer very, very quickly.

The journey to raise your children as their Courage Coach *and* parent will be a joyous one for you. Children are the largest and most rewarding puzzle you will ever assemble! By raising courageous children, you will build a foundation for your children to stand tall and be unique, as they live and express their positive attitude in this challenging world.

When you succeed—and you will—your disciplined, trustworthy, safe, and *golden* young adult will be in the minority among his or her *orange* (frustrated and damaged) peer group. What a tribute it will be when your child stands tall, recognized as the rare role model other parents want their children to emulate. Be prepared for the question to be asked: "How did you raise such a nice, brave kid during these unpredictable and dangerous times?" Your answer is honorable, if you choose to express it: "I decided to be more than a parent, I became a Courage Coach."

RESOURCES

Character Development

Aumiller, Gary, Ph.D. *Keeping It Simple: Sorting Out What Really Matters in Your Life*. Hauppauge, NY: Probity Press, 1995.

Beausay, William J. II. *Boys! Shaping Ordinary Boys into Extraordinary Men*. Nashville, TN: Thomas Nelson, Inc., 1994.

Benson, Herbert, M.D., and William Proctor. *The Break-Out Principle*. New York: Scribner, 2003.

Benson, Herbert, M.D. *Timeless Healing: The Power of Biology and Belief*. New York: Scribner, 1996.

Bluestein, Jane, Ph.D. *21st Century Discipline: Teaching Students Responsibility and Self-Control*. Jefferson City, MO: Scholastic, Inc., 1988.

Bower, Sharon Anthony, and Gordon H. Bower. *Asserting Yourself*. Reading, MA: Addison-Wesley Publishing, 1980.

Burnell, Ivan. *The Power of Positive Doing*. Center Ossipee, NH: International Personal Development, 1990.

Chopra, Deepak, M.D. *Unconditional Life: Discovering the Power to Fulfill Your Dreams*. New York: Bantam Books, 1991.

Cline, Foster, M.D., and Jim Fay. *Love and Logic Magic for Early Childhood: Practical Parenting from Birth to Six Years.* Golden, CO: Love & Logic Press, 2002.

Cline, Foster, M.D., and Jim Fay. *Parenting with Love and Logic: Teaching Children Responsibility.* Colorado Springs: Navpress, 1990.

Cline, Foster, M.D., and Jim Fay. *Parenting Teens with Love and Logic: Preparing Adolescents for Responsible Adulthood.* Colorado Springs: Navpress, 1993.

Conwell, Russell. *Acres of Diamonds.* Kansas City, MO: Hallmark Cards, Inc., 1968.

Cousins, Norman. *Head First: The Biology of Hope.* New York: E. P. Dutton, 1989.

Crim, Mort. *Second Thoughts: One Hundred Upbeat Messages for Beat-Up Americans.* Deerfield Beach, FL: Health Communications, Inc., 1997.

Csikszentmihalyi, Mihaly. *Becoming Adult: How Teenagers Prepare for the World of Work.* New York: Basic Books, 2000.

Csikszentmihalyi, Mihaly. *Creativity: Flow and the Psychology of Discovery and Invention.* New York: HarperCollins, 1996.

Csikszentmihalyi, Mihaly. *Talented Teenagers: The Roots of Success and Failure.* New York: Cambridge University Press, 2000.

Day, Laura. *Practical Intuition.* New York: Villard Books, 1996.

DePorter, Bobbi, and Mike Hernacki. *Quantum Learning.* New York: Dell, 1992.

Epstein, Fred, M.D., and Josh Horwitz. *If I Get to Five: What Children Can Teach Us About Courage and Character.* New York: Henry Holt & Company, 2003.

Friel, John C., Ph.D., and Linda D. Friel, M.A. *The 7 Worst Things Parents Do.* Deerfield Beach, FL: Health Communications, Inc., 1999.

Fritz, Robert. *The Path of Least Resistance: Learning to Become the Creative Force in Your Own Life.* New York: Fawcett Columbine, 1984.

Garbarino, James, Ph.D. *Lost Boys: Why Our Sons Turn Violent and How We Can Save Them.* New York: The Free Press, 1999.

Glasser, William, M.D. *The Quality School.* New York: Harper & Row, 1990.

Glasser, William, M.D. *Unhappy Teenagers: A Way for Parents and Teachers to Reach Them.* New York: HarperCollins, 2002.

Glassner, Barry. *The Culture of Fear.* New York: Basic Books, 1999.

Halberstam, Yitta, and Judith Leventhal. *Small Miracles: Extraordinary Coincidences from Everyday Life.* Holbrook, MA: Adams Media, 1997.

Kaufman, Gershen, Ph.D., Lev Raphael, Ph.D., and Pamela Espeland. *Stick Up for Yourself: Every Kid's Guide to Personal Power & Positive Self-Esteem.* Minneapolis: Free Spirit Publishing, 1999.

Kilbourne, Jean. *Deadly Persuasion: Why Women and Girls Must Fight the Addictive Power of Advertising.* New York: The Free Press, 1999.

Koehler, Michael, and Karen Royer. *First Class Character Education Activities Program: Ready to Use Lessons and Activities for Grades 7–12.* Hoboken, NJ: Jossey-Bass, 2002.

LaPierre, Wayne. *Guns, Crime and Freedom.* New York: Harper Perennial, 1995.

Markova, Dawna, Ph.D. *How Your Child Is Smart: A Life-Changing Approach to Learning.* Berkeley, CA: Conari Press, 1992.

Markova, Dawna, Ph.D. *Open Mind: Exploring Patterns of Natural Intelligence.* Berkeley, CA: Conari Press, 1996.

Rose, Colin, and Malcolm J. Nicholl. *Accelerated Learning for the 21st Century.* New York: Delacorte Press, 1997.

Senge, Peter M. *The Fifth Discipline.* New York: Currency Doubleday, 1990.

Tallard-Johnson, Julie. *Celebrate You! Building Your Self-Esteem.* Minneapolis, MN: Lerner Publications, 1991.

Thomas, Bob, and Greg Lewis. *Good Sports: Making Sports a Positive Experience for Everyone.* Grand Rapids, MI: Zondervan Publishing House, 1994.

Wonder, Jacquelyn, and Priscilla Donovan. *Whole-Brain Thinking.* New York: Quill William Morrow, 1984.

Communication Skills

Acosta, Judith, LCSW, and Judith Simon Prager, Ph.D. *The Worst Is Over.* San Diego: Jodere Group, 2002.

Andreas, Connirae, Ph.D, and Steve Andreas, M.A. *Heart of the Mind.* Moab, UT: Real People Press, 1989.

Bandler, Richard, and John LaValle. *Persuasion Engineering*. Capitola, CA: Meta Publications, 1996.

Cappello, Dominic. *Ten Talks Parents Must Have with Their Children About Violence*. New York: Hyperion, 2000.

Cialdini, Robert B., Ph.D. *Influence: The New Psychology of Modern Persuasion*. New York: Quill, 1984.

Dawson, Roger. *Secrets of Power Persuasion*. Englewood Cliffs, NJ: Prentice Hall, 1992.

Decker, Bert. *You've Got to Be Believed to Be Heard*. New York: St. Martin's Press, 1992.

Elgin, Suzette Haden. *The Gentle Art of Verbal Self-Defense*. New York: Dorset Press, 1980.

Elgin, Suzette Haden. *How to Turn the Other Cheek and Still Survive in Today's World*. Nashville, TN: Thomas Nelson Publishers, 1997.

Elgin, Suzette Haden. *The Last Word on the Gentle Art of Verbal Self-Defense*. New York: Prentice Hall Press, 1987.

Elgin, Suzette Haden. *Success with the Gentle Art of Verbal Self-Defense*. Englewood Cliffs, NJ: Prentice Hall, 1989.

Horn, Sam. *Take the Bully by the Horns: Stop Unethical, Uncooperative, or Unpleasant People from Running and Ruining Your Life*. New York: St. Martin's Press, 2002.

Horn, Sam. *Tongue Fu*. New York: St. Martin's Press, 1996.

Jacobs, Donald Trent. *Patient Communication for First Responders and EMS Personnel*. Englewood Cliffs, NJ, 1991.

Laborde, Genie Z. *Influencing with Integrity*. Palo Alto, CA: Syntony Publishing, 1997.

Levine, Robert, Ph.D. *The Power of Persuasion*. Hoboken, NJ: John Wiley & Sons, 2003.

Lieberman, David J., Ph.D. *Never Be Lied to Again*. New York: St. Martin's Press, 1998.

Linden, Anne. *Mindworks: NLP Tools for Building a Better Life*. New York: Berkley Books, 1997.

Massey, Morris. *The People Puzzle: Understanding Yourself and Others*. Reston, VA: Reston Publishing, 1979.

Mayhall, Carole. *Words That Hurt, Words That Heal*. Colorado Springs: NavPress, 1986.

McMaster, Michael, and John Grinder. *Precision: A New Approach to Communication*. Bonny Doon, CA: Precision Models, 1980.

Moorman, Chick. *Talk Sense to Yourself: The Language of Personal Power*. Portage, MI: Personal Power Press, 1985.

Perry, J. Mitchell, Ph.D., and Richard E. Griggs. *The Road to Optimism: Change Your Language—Change Your Life!* San Ramon, CA: Manfit Press, 1997.

Robbins, Anthony. *Awaken the Giant Within*. New York: Summit Books, 1991.

Robbins, Anthony. *Unlimited Power*. New York: Simon & Schuster, 1986.

Rushkoff, Douglas. *Coercion: Why We Listen to What "They" Say*. New York: Riverhead Books, 1999.

Scott, Susan. *Fierce Conversations*. New York: Penguin Group, 2002.

Seligman, Martin. *Authentic Happiness*. New York: The Free Press, 2002.

Thompson, George J., Ph.D., and Jerry B. Jenkins. *Verbal Judo*. New York: William Morrow and Company, 1993.

Van Fleet, James K. *The Complete Guide to Verbal Manipulation*. Paramus, NJ: Prentice Hall, 1984.

Van Fleet, James K. *25 Steps to Power and Mastery over People*. West Nyack, NY: Parker Publications, 1983.

Walter, Otis M., and Robert L. Scott. *Thinking and Speaking*. New York: The Macmillan Company, 1962.

Walther, George R. *Power Talking*. New York: Berkley Books, 1991.

York, Marian. *The Loving Dictionary: 1,001 Words of Appreciation to Energize, Enrich and Empower All of Your Relationships*. Seattle, WA: 1st Books Library, 2001.

Courage Story Books for Young Children

Cooper-Mullin, Alison. *Once Upon a Heroine*. New York: McGraw-Hill, 1998 (girls ages 2 to 14).

Emberley, Ed. *Go Away, Big Green Monster*. New York: Little, Brown and Company, 1993 (all ages).

Henkes, Kevin. *Sheila Rae, the Brave*. New York: Harper Trophy, 1996 (ages 4 to 8).

Hubbard, Woodleigh Marx. *All That You Are*. New York: Putnam Publishing Group, 2000 (ages 4 to 8).

Jones, Rebecca C. *Down at the Bottom of the Deep Dark Sea*. New York: Simon & Schuster, 1991 (ages 4 to 6).

Mallat, Kathy. *Brave Bear*. New York: Walker and Company, 2001 (ages 2 to 4).

Mann, Kenny. *I Am Not Afraid*. Milwaukee, WI: Gareth Stevens, 1997 (ages 4 to 8).

Mayer, Mercer. *There's a Nightmare in My Closet*. London: Puffin Books, 1992 (ages 4 to 8).

Millman, Dan. *Secret of the Peaceful Warrior*. Novato, CA: HJ Kramer, 1991 (ages 5 to 8).

Piper, Watty. *The Little Engine That Could*. New York: Grosset & Dunlap, 1978 (ages 4 to 8).

Sendak, Maurice. *Where the Wild Things Are*. New York: Harper Collins, 1988 (ages 4 to 8).

Sperry, Armstrong. *Call It Courage*. Reading, MA: Scott Foresman, 1990 (ages 5 to 8).

Steig, William. *Brave Irene*. New York: Farrar, Strauss and Giroux, 1986 (ages 3 to 8).

Williams, Linda. *The Little Old Lady Who Was Not Afraid of Anything*. New York: Harper Trophy, 1988 (ages 5 to 8).

Wormell, Mary. *Hilda Hen's Scary Night*. San Diego: Harcourt, 1996 (ages 4 to 6).

Courageous True Stories for Teens

Coffee, Gerald. *Beyond Survival: A POW's Inspiring Lesson in Living*. New York: Putnam, 1991.

Graham, Billy. *Your Ship Came In the Day the Doctor Smacked Your Bum: A Motivational Memoir*. Auckland, New Zealand: Hodder Moa Beckett, 1998.

Johnson, Beth. *Everyday Heroes*. West Berlin, NJ: Townsend Press, 1996.

Karnes, Frances, Ph.D. *Girls and Young Women*. Minneapolis: Free Spirit, 1993.

Kersey, Cynthia. *Unstoppable: 45 Powerful Stories of Perseverance and Triumph from People Just Like You*. Naperville, IL: Sourcebooks, Inc., 1998.

MacPherson, Malcolm. *On a Wing and a Prayer*. New York: Harper Collins, 2002.

Maron, Linda. *Rescue 911*. New York: Berkley Books, 1993.

O'Grady, Scott. *Basher Five-Two*. New York: Bantam Doubleday Dell, 1997.

O'Grady, Scott. *Return with Honor*. New York: Harper Torch, 1996.

Pflug, Jackie Nink. *Miles to Go Before I Sleep*. Center City, MN: Hazelden Information Education, 2002.

Plumb, Charlie. *I'm No Hero: A POW Story as Told to Glen DeWerff*. Calabasas, CA: Executive Books, 1995.

Read, Piers Paul. *Alive*. New York: Avon Books, 1974.

Schemmel, Jerry. *Chosen to Live*. Littleton, CO: Victory Publishing, 1996.

Smith, Bobby E. *Visions of Courage*. LaGrange, GA: Four Winds Publishing, 1998.

Defense Tactics (Mental, Verbal, and Physical)

Bishop, Bob, and Matt Thomas. *Protecting Children from Danger*. Berkeley, CA: North Atlantic Books, 1993.

Bloomfield, Harold H., M.D., and Robert K.Cooper, Ph.D. *How to Be Safe in an Unsafe World*. New York: Crown Publishers, 1997.

Byrnes, John D. *Before Conflict: Preventing Aggressive Behavior*. Lanham, MD: Rowman and Littlefield, 2002.

Danto, Bruce L., M.D. *Prime Target*. Philadelphia: The Charles Press, 1990.

DeBecker, Gavin. *The Gift of Fear*. Boston: Little, Brown and Company, 1997.

Gardner, Debbie. *Simply the BST Crime Survival*. Mansfield. OH: Bookmasters, 2002.

Gardner, Debbie. *Survive: Don't be a Victim!* New York: Warner Books, 1982.

Grossman, Dave, Lt. Col. *On Killing*. Boston: Little, Brown and Company, 1995.

Grossman, Dave, Lt. Col., and Gloria DeGaetano. *Stop Teaching Our Kids to Kill*. New York: Crown Publications, 1999.

Hibbard, Jack, and Bryan A. Fried. *Weaponless Defense*. Springfield, IL: Charles C. Thomas, 1980.

Lee, Bruce. *The Tao of Jeet Kune Do*. Burbank, CA: Ohara Publications, 1975.

Lovette, Ed, and Dave Spaulding. *Defensive Living: Street Proven Wisdom*. Flushing, NY: Looseleaf Law Publications, 2000.

Peters, John G. *Realistic Defensive Tactics*. Albuquerque, NM: Reliapon Police Products, 1981.

Prothrow-Stith, Deborah, M.D. *Deadly Consequences: How Violence Is Destroying Our Teenage Population and a Plan to Begin Solving the Problem*. New York: HarperCollins, 1991.

Rail, Robert R. *Defense without Damage*. Upland, PA: Diane Publishing, 1994.

Redenbach, Robert, and Albertus Wessels. *Kontact*. Victoria, Australia: Global Security Training, 1994.

Remsberg, Charles. *The Tactical Edge: Surviving High Risk Patrol*. Northbrook, IL: Calibre Press, 1986.

Trump, Kenneth S. *Classroom Killers? Hallway Hostages? How Schools Can Prevent and Manage School Crises*. Thousand Oaks, CA: Corwin Press, 2000.

Trump, Kenneth S. *Practical School Security: Basic Guidelines for Safe and Secure Schools*. Thousand Oaks, CA: Corwin Press, 1998.

Vila, Bryan. *Tired Cops: The Importance of Managing Police Fatigue*. Washington, DC: Police Executive Research Forum, 2000.

Weeks, Dudley, Ph.D. *The Eight Essential Steps to Conflict Resolution*. Los Angeles: Jeremy P. Tarcher, Inc., 1992.

Wooden, John, Coach, and Steve Jamison. *Wooden: A Lifetime of Observations and Reflections On and Off the Court*. Chicago: Contemporary Books, 1997.

Ziglar, Zig. *Raising Positive Kids in a Negative World*. Nashville, TN: Oliver-Nelson Books, 1985.

Peak Performance and Decision-Making under Stress

Artwohl, Alexis, Ph.D., and Loren Christensen. *Deadly Force Encounters: What Cops Need to Know to Mentally and Physically Prepare for and Survive a Gunfight.* Boulder, CO: Paladin Press, 1997.

Blum, Lawrence N., Ph.D. *Force under Pressure: How Cops Live and Why They Die.* New York: Lantern Books, 2000.

Blum, Lawrence N., Ph.D. *Stoning the Keepers at the Gate.* New York: Lantern Books, 2002.

Butler, Gillian, Ph.D., and Tony Hope, M.D. *Managing Your Mind: The Mental Fitness Guide.* New York: Oxford University Press, 1995.

Cannon-Bowers, Janis A. *Making Decisions under Stress: Implications for Individual & Team Training.* Washington, DC: American Psychological Association, 2000.

Childre, Doc Lew. *Cut-Thru: Achieve Total Security and Maximum Energy.* Boulder Creek, CA: Planetary Publications, 1996.

Childre, Doc Lew. *Freeze Frame.* Boulder Creek, CA: Planetary Publications, 1994.

Childre, Doc Lew, and Howard Martin. *The HeartMath Solution.* San Francisco: HarperSanFrancisco, 1999.

Cooper, Robert K., Ph.D. *The Performance Edge.* Boston: Houghton Mifflin Company, 1991.

Dorfman, H. A., and Karl Kuehil. *The Mental Game of Baseball: A Guide to Peak Performance.* South Bend, IN: Diamond Communications, Inc., 1995.

Gilmartin, Kevin M., Ph.D. *Emotional Survival for Law Enforcement.* Tucson, AZ: E-S Press, 2002.

Glasser, William, M.D. *Take Effective Control of Your Life.* New York: Harper & Row, 1984.

Greene, Don, Ph.D. *Fight Your Fear and Win.* New York: Broadway Books, 2001.

Hall, Doug. *Making the Courage Connection.* New York: Fireside, 1997.

Hall, Doug. *The Maverick Mindset: Finding the Courage to Journey from Fear to Freedom.* New York: Simon & Schuster, 1997.

Hammond, Kenneth R. *Judgments under Stress.* New York: Oxford University Press, 2000.

Hammond, John S. *Smart Choices: A Practical Guide to Making Better Decisions*. New York: Broadway, 2002.

Hansen, Mark Victor. *Dare to Win*. Newport Beach, CA: Mark Victor Hansen, 1988.

Hoke, James H. *I Would If I Could and I Can*. New York: Stein and Day, 1980.

Horn, Sam. *Concrete Confidence*. New York: St. Martin's Press, 1997.

Hunt, Morton. *The Compassionate Beast: What Science Is Discovering about the Humane Side of Humankind*. New York: William Morrow, 1990.

Klein, Gary. *Sources of Power: How People Make Decisions*. Cambridge, MA: MIT Press, 1999.

Krebs, Dennis, Kenneth Henry, and Mark Gabriele. *When Violence Erupts: A Survival Guide for Emergency Responders*. St. Louis, MO: C. V. Mosby Company, 1990.

LeBoeuf, Michael, Ph.D. *Getting Results: The Secret to Motivating Yourself and Others*. New York: Berkley Books, 1985.

Leonard, George. *The Ultimate Athlete*. Berkeley, CA: North Atlantic Books, 1974.

Loehr, James. *Toughness Training for Life*. New York: Penguin Books, 1993.

Loehr, James, and Jeffrey Migdow, M.D. *Breathe In, Breathe Out*. Alexandria, VA: Time Life Books, 1986.

Loehr, James, and Tony Schwartz. *The Power of Full Engagement: Managing Energy, Not Time, Is the Key to High Performance and Personal Renewal*. New York: The Free Press, 2003.

Lofland, Donald, Ph.D. *Thought Viruses*. New York: Harmony Books, 1997.

Markova, Dawna, Ph.D. *I Will Not Die an Unlived Life*. York Beach, ME: Conari Press, 2000.

Moore, Jim. *First You Slay the Dragon*. Coppel, TX: Moore Ideas, Inc., 1997.

Murphy, Shane, Ph.D. *The Achievement Zone*. New York: G. P. Putnam's Sons, 1996.

Noe, John R. *Peak Performance Principles for High Achievers*. New York: Berkley Books, 1984.

Pearsall, Paul, Ph.D. *The Beethoven Factor: The New Positive Psychology of Hardiness, Happiness, Healing and Hope*. Charlottesville, VA: Hampton Roads Publishing, 2003.

Pearsall, Paul, Ph.D. *The Heart's Code*. New York: Broadway, 1998.

Pelletier, Kenneth R. *Mind as Healer, Mind as Slayer*. New York: Dell Publishing, 1977.

Pelletier, Ray. *Permission to Win*. Akron, OH: Oakhill Press, 1997.

Perry, J. Mitchell, Ph.D., and Steve Jamison. *In The Zone: Achieving Optimal Performance in Business—as in Sports*. Chicago: Contemporary Books, 1997.

Plous, Scott. *The Psychology of Judgment and Decision Making*. New York: McGraw-Hill, 1993.

Restak, Richard, M.D. *Mozart's Brain and the Fighter Pilot: Unleashing Your Brain's Potential*. New York: Harmony Books, 2001.

Rohn, E. James. *The Five Major Pieces to the Life Puzzle*. Dallas: Great Impressions, 1991.

Schmidt, Richard A. *Motor Learning & Performance: From Principles to Practice*. Champaign, IL: Human Kinetics Books, 1991.

Selleck, George A., Ph.D. *How to Play the Game of Your Life*. South Bend, IN: Diamond Communications, 1995.

Siddle, Bruce K. *Sharpening the Warrior's Edge*. Millstad, IL: PPCT Research Publications, 1995.

Sugarman, Karlene, M.A. *Winning the Mental Way*. Burlingame, CA: Step Up Publishing, 1999.

Waitley, Denis. *The Psychology of Winning*. Chicago: Nightengale-Conant Corp., 1979.

Walsh, Roger, M.D. *Staying Alive: The Psychology of Human Survival*. Boston: Shambhala Publications, 1984.

Wrenn, C. Gilbert. *The Mind Benders*. Circle Pines, MN: American Guidance Service, 1971.

Movies with Courage Themes

* Note: You should view these movies on your own first, determining if the material is age-appropriate for your child.

Alive / Alive: 20 years later documentary

Apollo 13

Billy Elliott

Billy Jack
Braveheart
Courage Under Fire
ET
Glory
A Few Good Men
Finding Nemo
Gladiator
Happy Gilmore
Karate Kid
Little Giants
Lord of the Rings Trilogy
The Patriot
Pay It Forward
Rocky
The Sandlot
Seabiscuit
Spiderman
Titanic
Without Limits

Courage Supplies

BOB—Body Opponent Bag and Base

A great partner for allowing your children to strike the throat. BOB, Century's Body Opponent Bag, is a full-size lifelike mannequin. BOB has two height adjustments, from 5 feet, 6 inches to 6 feet tall. The polyethylene base can be filled with sand or water and is rounded for easy roll relocation. BOB weighs approximately 270 pounds when filled. Besides being used for physical practice, BOB serves as an excellent visual reminder of your courage coaching. You can dress BOB up for family events (Halloween, parties, and so on). BOB is available at most major sporting goods stores throughout the United States.

Kubotan Key Holder

Grand Master Takayuki Kubota originally invented the Kubotan to be used by police officers. The Kubotan is a hard plastic cylinder about

5½ inches long and ⁹⁄₁₆ inch in diameter and has a key ring attached. Kubotans are available at police supply stores across the United States and on the Internet.

SEND POLICE Car Banner

The 36 × 8-inch fluorescent orange sign with black lettering (SEND POLICE) includes two (2) suction cups. It attaches to the inside or outside rear window of a car, van, or truck during an emergency and asks all passing vehicles to notify the police and report your emergency. SEND POLICE banners are very difficult to find. SEND POLICE is a specific command that police respond to the scene. Simply asking passing motorists to Call Police does not give the dispatcher any direction. Make sure your banner says, SEND POLICE. You can make your own SEND POLICE banners or get information from www.surviveinstitute.com

INDEX

About the Authors

Debbie and **Mike Gardner** met in the Cincinnati Police Academy over 30 years ago. Debbie spent 8 years as a deputy sheriff with the Hamilton County Sheriff's Office. Mike spent 27 years with the Cincinnati Police Department, serving 7 of those years as a training sergeant at the Cincinnati Police Academy. After leaving the Cincinnati Police Department, Mike served as the training captain in the Warren County Sheriff's Office, just north of Cincinnati. They had extensive training during their distinguished law enforcement careers.

They are the founders of the Survive Institute, an organization dedicated to courage-based personal protection seminars, and their client list includes the Federal Bureau of Investigation, U.S. Army, California Prison Guards, Procter & Gamble, General Motors, Ford Motor Company, Kelly Services, 3M, Internal Revenue Service, Meeting Planners International, American Society of Association Executives, Young Presidents Organization, and more. They have been featured on various TV shows and radio programs and in magazines and newspapers throughout the United States, Canada, Australia, Europe, and South America.

Debbie and Mike have been married since 1975 and have two children, Jaclyn and Jimmy.